First Day to Final Grade

THIRD EDITION

First Day to Final Grade

THIRD EDITION

A Graduate Student's Guide to Teaching

Anne Curzan and Lisa Damour

Ann Arbor
The University of Michigan Press

ISBN-13: 978-0-472-03451-2

2017   2016   2015   6   5   4

Contents

Introduction

This book is designed to be an accessible, pragmatic teaching guide on a wide range of issues that arise both inside and outside the classroom for many first-time teaching assistants. The advice stems not only from our own experiences in the classroom but also from extensive consultation with other experienced teaching assistants as well as university faculty in a variety of disciplines who are highly regarded for their teaching skills. Important principles in pedagogical theory underlie much of the material presented here, and all our advice is grounded in broader pedagogical approaches. But our focus remains on the practical, day-to-day matters you will face as a teaching assistant and how you can approach them effectively.

Graduate students teaching in university settings face unique issues in the classroom. Much of the material in this book will be helpful to new teachers at other stages in their careers, but some of the material is aimed directly at new graduate student teachers.

We strongly recommend that you familiarize yourself with the excellent material published on pedagogy in higher education, and we offer suggested readings throughout this book. We also recognize that not all theoretical material on pedagogy aims to provide practical advice (on such banal matters as when to do your photocopying); we offer this book as a complementary resource for first-time teaching assistants. There is great value to theoretical material about teaching; there is also great value to practical advice.

The kind of collaboration that has created this book is one of the keys to successful teaching at every level. We all develop as teachers throughout our careers as we learn from our own experiences as well as the experiences of others. Much of this collaboration happens informally—over lunch or during a chance meeting in the hallway. Some of it happens more formally during pedagogical workshops or training sessions. In this book, we have tried to record a range of teaching wisdom so that first-time teachers will have immediate access to a teaching resource when there is no workshop planned and the hallways are empty.

▣ Organization of the Book

Each topic in this book is divided into headings and subheadings for easy reference. The Contents and Index will help you locate exactly what you need at any given point (or moment of crisis) during the term.

Each chapter includes explanations and examples, from handouts to conversations. Appendixes at the end of the book include longer exemplary documents. In each chapter, we also share teaching anecdotes that we have collected to help you realize that whatever happens to you (especially if it is embarrassing or painful) something similar, if not worse, has happened to someone else. These appear in boldfaced type and are set off near the margins. At the end of each chapter you will find a short list of possible further readings should you wish to pursue a particular topic; we have limited these references to generally relevant books, many of which contain excellent bibliographies with more specifically directed books and articles.

▣ Terminology

Teaching Assistant

Graduate students at different universities prefer different terms for referring to their teaching role in the classroom: teaching assistant, graduate student instructor, graduate instructor, and so on. We had to pick one, and we settled on *teaching assistant*. There are connotation problems with *teaching assistant,* the most important of which is that it implies that the graduate student is necessarily helping a professor to teach, which is not always the case. Many graduate students run their own courses, and even those who run a section for a larger lecture course are still teaching on their own. The term *teaching assistant* is, however, the most widely accepted and used term for graduate students who teach; we hope no one will take offense at the selection of this term.

Singular Generic *They*

In writing general material about teaching assistants and students, it is impossible to avoid the "generic pronoun problem." Luckily, Anne has devoted (frighteningly) many research hours to this subject and, for better or worse, has strong views on the matter. Lisa, a psychologist, deferred to Anne, the linguist, entirely on this matter. Please send all contrary responses on this subject straight to Anne.

English does have a generic singular pronoun: it is *they*, and most of us use it in spoken language all the time. Grammar books finally have accepted that "generic *he*" is not generic, which leaves us with the "acceptable" option of *he or she*, but that can sound awkward (and it would make this book longer!). Grammarians state that while using *they* with a singular subject might create gender agreement, it violates number agreement. Not necessarily so. The pronoun *they* has taken on a singular function with singular subjects of unknown gender, and English speakers and readers are rarely significantly confused about the number of people in question (this change is not without precedence: *you*, formerly only plural, took on a singular function). We have opted, therefore, to be on the cutting edge of written language change, to stick to our guns, and to use singular *they*.

The Authors

Lisa Damour received a B.A. in psychology from Yale in 1992 and a Ph.D. in clinical psychology from the University of Michigan in May 1997. With all her newfound free time (if we ignore that she then started a postdoctoral fellowship), she decided to write a book with her friend and squash/swimming/running partner, Anne. Lisa worked as a teaching assistant for six semesters at the University of Michigan. She now has a private practice in Cleveland and is an adjunct faculty member at John Carroll University and a clinical instructor at Case Western Reserve University.

Anne Curzan received a B.A. in linguistics from Yale in 1991 and a Ph.D. in English from the University of Michigan in June 1998. To "complement" the work of writing her dissertation, she decided to write a book with her friend and squash/swimming/running partner, Lisa. Anne taught English for two years at a university in central China after graduating from college; she worked as a teaching assistant for six semesters at the University of Michigan and received the David and Linda Moscow Award for Excellence in the Teaching of Composition. She is now Associate Professor of English at the University of Michigan.

Since 2003, Lisa and Anne have been invited by the organizers of T.A. training programs around the country to present workshops or organize full programs for graduate student instructors.

▨ Changes to the Third Edition

One of the real joys of teaching and working with new teachers is that we continue to refine our own practice of college teaching and how we think about introducing that practice to new teachers. This edition of *First Day to Final Grade* incorporates what we have learned since the second edition was published in 2006. This edition also includes two major additions.

First, we have added a new chapter titled Preparing for the Job Market, which helps prepare teaching assistants to apply for academic jobs, both in terms of creating a teaching portfolio and preparing for job interviews. Second, we have tried to account for some of the notable changes in college teaching that have emerged since the publication of the last edition, including the pervasive use of technology in all aspects of teaching, the growing number of college students whose mental health issues affect our teaching, and the increasing role of students' parents in some of our interactions with students.

As was the case with the second edition, many of the changes that we've made for this new edition have grown out of our direct work with graduate student instructors at our home schools and at the universities where we have conducted T.A. training workshops or programs. We welcome the chance to grapple with the range and variety of challenges that face graduate student instructors and feel grateful for their willingness to share their experiences with us.

▨ Acknowledgments

This book would not have been possible without the help and support of so many of our friends, colleagues, and mentors. In particular we would like to thank Eileen Anderson-Fye, Matt Baker, James Beitler, Mary and Mike Curzan, Kate Gjaja, Karen Glennemeier, Johns Hopkins, Emily Hoyer, Darren Keefe, the late Glen Knudsvig, Mark Koch, Rosemary Kowalski, Nathan Kutz, Zak Lancaster, Sumati Murli, Chris Peterson, and Terri Tinkle for their time, meticulous reading, and invaluable comments on earlier versions of the manuscript. Special thanks also go to Doug Burger, Susan Montgomery, Fran Smith, and John Whittier-Ferguson, who all provided experienced advice on a multitude of teaching issues; to our students and instructors, who have taught us what it means to teach; and to Joel Smith, who provided, from the beginning, the backing that allowed our idea to become a book. Our families have given us unflagging support, counsel, and love throughout the process, and our friends have provided us with a never-ending supply of ideas and memorable quotes about teaching. For all of this and more, we are immeasurably grateful.

1

Becoming a Teacher

Welcome to being a graduate student teaching assistant! Your mission is to enhance the education of undergraduate students. This is a challenging and exciting task that is often tinged with anxiety for first-time teachers.

While most graduate students are both eager to teach and nervous about teaching, universities have been slow to provide adequate training programs for first-time teachers. Stepping into the breach, we have written this book so you do not feel that you are starting from scratch. You will learn from your own experiences in the classroom, but we hope that the information in this book will spare you from repeating mistakes that others have already made.

> "The only advice I got before I started teaching was to erase the board using vertical strokes: erasing the board from side to side makes your butt wiggle."

Your department may or may not view your teaching responsibilities as a priority compared to your research and course work. But you should take this job seriously: you have been entrusted with the education of undergraduate students, which is a critical contribution to your department and to your field as a whole.

This chapter will supply some general advice about what to do once you find yourself in a classroom.

▣ Your Teaching Persona

Teaching is a kind of performance, and the person you are in the front of a classroom is in some ways different from the person you are outside of it. Developing your *teaching persona*—the person you become once you step into the classroom—takes time and experience.

Finding Your Teaching Persona

Over time, you will discover whether you, as an instructor, are loud or quiet, funny or serious, a sitter or a stander, a board user or a handout maven. In the meantime, experiment with different approaches until you figure out what feels comfortable and what elicits the best reaction from your students. Don't hesitate to try something that may not "feel like you," because your teaching persona may turn out to be an unexpected side of you. But do not be afraid to reject suggestions on teaching that you feel your innate personality will prevent you from pulling off (e.g., singing mnemonic devices). You will look uncomfortable and be less effective.

Teaching with Authority

For beginning teachers, there is often a progression from *acting like* you are in charge of the classroom to *feeling like* you are in charge of the classroom. This is normal. Unless you give them reason not to, students will generally accept your authority no matter how you feel about your qualifications as a teacher.

You will start to *feel* like you are in charge of your classroom as you gain experience. Until then, you may find that you rely more on "the rules" (guidelines, due dates, syllabi) and on established teacher-student roles to create a feeling of authority. For example, many teaching assistants start by imitating favorite teachers of their own. As you get more experience and confidence, you will be able to act more natural in your

> "As a college student, I was taught by a teaching assistant who looked like she was thirteen years old. Although she looked so young, her confidence, competence, and terrific preparation for class earned everybody's respect by the end of the first meeting."

role as an instructor. You then will be better able to be more like yourself while you are teaching.

The Joys of Teaching

While teaching is an additional burden for already busy graduate students, there are several significant pleasures to being a teacher.

Giving Back

Teaching allows you to help other students learn and grow. It also reminds you that you already have a great deal to contribute to the teaching in your field, even if you still have a long way to go in your own education. You spend a lot of your time as a student focused on what you don't know; teaching helps you remember how much you do know.

Improving Your Own Studies

Teaching helps you to be a better student. You will become more receptive to the efforts of your own professors after you have been on the other side of the desk. Teaching also requires you to learn material more thoroughly than you ever learned it as a student.

Preparing for Your Career

Teaching as a graduate student offers excellent training to those who will go on to become professional teachers. It helps you become comfortable in the classroom and discover your own teaching style.

Expanding Your World

The life of a graduate student can be startlingly narrow. Many graduate students find that most of their time is spent doing very focused research and interacting with a relatively small number of colleagues. Teaching allows you to meet people at the university who are not your classmates or your professors. In addition, it can be a pleasure to feel that you are gainfully employed, even while you are pursuing your own course of studies.

Enjoying the Job

Teaching can be fun in and of itself. It allows you to be creative and enthusiastic. The chance to explore material in your field and your students' curiosity can also fuel your enthusiasm about your own research and your field in general.

◼ The Agonies of Teaching

At some point in your teaching career, you will fall flat on your face. It will probably happen more than once. It may be painful, but you will survive. And you should find it reassuring to know that *every* instructor has had this experience.

Bad Days ✓

You can come to class feeling completely prepared to teach brilliantly and leave wishing you had never gotten out of bed. Take some time to try to figure out what went wrong. Keep notes; you might teach the same course again several years later, and you usually know what you could have done better as soon as you leave the classroom. Learn from this experience, but do not torture yourself about it. Focus on making the next class better.

See pages 200–2 in Chapter 9, Meta-Teaching, for more information on what to do after a bad day.

Bad Courses

This happens. Some classes never gel; the professor organizes the course poorly; the course tries to cover too much or too difficult material; and/or you are not doing your best teaching for personal reasons. It is unfortunate when this happens, and all that you can do is try to figure out what went wrong and how you can improve things the next time.

Bad Class Dynamics

Any teaching assistant with more than one section at a time can attest that some sections work well and some do not. Your first reaction may be to blame yourself when a section does not go well, but also remember that the students play a key role in an effective classroom too. It may help to try adjusting your teaching style to a particular group of students, but there will always be groups of students who never come together.

Bad Teaching

Your car broke down. A relationship ended. You were up until 3:00 AM grading. You have had five cups of coffee, and you still *cannot* wake up. You will have bad days. It is your responsibility to do your best not to allow outside factors to bring down your teaching. When you teach badly, figure out how you can take care of yourself so that you are in better shape when it is time to teach again. Obsessing about what went wrong will not get you on the road to feeling (and teaching) better.

Maintaining Perspective

If you take teaching seriously, it can become almost life consuming. Class preparation and grading can take up as much time as you allow. And you can wrap up too much of your self-image in your performance as an instructor. A good teaching day can put you on an affirming high, and a bad teaching day can ruin your week. Cherish the highs (they can be a rare treat in graduate school), and focus on reacting productively to the lows.

What Your Students Are Thinking after Class

While you may spend the rest of the week worrying about whether or not your discussion was as lively as last week or whether the diagram you drew on the board was confusing, your students are not worrying about your class as much as you are. Most students are more focused on grasping the content of the material than on observing how you teach it. Additionally, undergraduates also have many other things on their minds besides your course (e.g., the exam they have that afternoon, their attraction to another student in your class). Some students will think about the class after they leave, but if the class did not go well, they may be as likely to attribute responsibility to themselves or to their classmates as they are to you. Try to remember this when you find yourself overly worried about how the class is working.

> **"One night at the supermarket, I wheeled my cart into the check-out line right behind one of my students. She looked completely shocked. She clearly believed that I did not exist outside the classroom."**

What You Should Be Thinking after Class

An important part of teaching is learning from experience. When a class goes well, think about what went right so that you can repeat it. When a class goes badly, think about what went wrong but do not kick yourself about it; just fix it. See it as a learning experience, not as a statement about your ultimate abilities as a teacher. Most mistakes can be fixed in the next class. Remember that a bad class session does not make a bad course.

Care about your students and their learning. Also, be kind to yourself: remember that you are still learning too.

⊞ **Further Reading**

Allen, R. R., and T. Rueter. 1990. *Teaching Assistant Strategies.* Dubuque, IA: Kendall/Hunt.

Darley, J. M., Zanna, M. O., and H. L. Roediger, eds. 2003. *The Compleat Academic: A Career Guide.* 2d ed. Washington, DC: American Psychological Association.

Davis, B. G. 2009. *Tools for Teaching.* 2d ed. San Francisco: Jossey-Bass.

Eble, K. 1988. *The Craft of Teaching.* 2d ed. San Francisco: Jossey-Bass.

Rotenberg, R. 2010. *The Art and Craft of College Teaching: A Guide for New Professors and Graduate Students.* 2d ed. Walnut Creek, CA: Left Coast Press.

Svinicki, M., and W. J. McKeachie. 2011. *McKeachie's Teaching Tips: Strategies, Research, and Theory for College and University Teachers.* 13th ed. Belmont, CA: Wadsworth.

Tice, S. L., Jackson, N., Lambert, L. M., and P. Englot, eds. 2005. *University Teaching: A Reference Guide for Graduate Students and Faculty.* 2d ed. Syracuse, NY: Syracuse University Press.

2

The First Day of the Term

The first day of teaching, whether it is your first day ever or just the first day of the term, is a simultaneously exhilarating and terrifying experience. You do not know the students, and you want to make a good first impression. You may not be sure of the course logistics, yet you want to sound like you are. This chapter will help you plan for and survive your first day with as little stress as possible.

> "I think the day I stop getting nervous before the first day of class—and even a little nervous and 'adrenalined' before every class—may be the day I stop growing as a teacher."

Before Classes Begin

Here is a short checklist to help you avoid many potential "first day" headaches.

Know Your Students ✓

If you can get the class list ahead of time, begin to familiarize yourself with the students' names. You will have an easier time remembering names if you already have a sense of them. If you cannot get a class list in advance, find out how many students you should expect so that you will know how many chairs you will need and how many copies of handouts to make.

Some universities now provide instructors with photo rosters, so that you can start associating names with faces. However, be aware that some students will bear little to no resemblance to their ID photo.

Check Your Classroom ✓

Look at the classroom before your first class meeting. First of all, you want to be sure you know where it is. Getting lost on the way to class can take all of the fun out of your first day of teaching. Second, you need to know how the chairs are arranged and whether they can be moved; where the board is and whether it comes with chalk, pens, and an eraser; whether there is a table or podium, and so on. This way, you can be realistic when you think about the logistics of the first day. And you can be sure to have at least as many chairs as you have students.

Check Class Start Times ✓

At some universities, classes actually begin ten (or more) minutes after the time printed in the course schedule to allow students time to get from one class to the next. Check to see if such a policy exists at your university.

Meet the Administrative Staff

Find out which administrator is responsible for the teaching of undergraduates in your department, and make a point of meeting them and their staff. It will prove immensely useful later in the term if you know and are on friendly terms with the director of undergraduate studies, the supervisor of all of the chemistry labs, or the coordinator of the introductory language program. You may look to this person for advice or intervention in a difficult situation, and it helps if they already know who you are.

Administrative staff in the department wield much of the bureaucratic clout, so (common decency aside) you would do well to be polite and friendly in your interactions with them. Staff can often make a room change, arrange an equipment loan, or honor and even expedite another teaching request if you ask nicely. They also are often the source of invaluable advice.

Develop Your Class Plan

Create a detailed class plan. The more detail you put into the plan, the more confident you will feel walking into the classroom. Think about what you are going to say at the start of class, and practice it in front of a mirror. It sounds silly to practice your opening, but you have a better shot at delivering it effectively if you have done it before.

See pages 32–37 in Chapter 3, The Lesson Plan, for more information on writing lesson plans.

Do Your Copying

Make copies of all the syllabi and handouts that you will need. Do not leave this task until the day of your first class because there are always a lot of people making copies at the start of the term. There either will be a huge line or the copier will have gotten tired and decided to stop working.

Some instructors post the syllabus on the course management system before the first day of class. If you will not be providing copies of the syllabus, alert students that it is on the course management system and plan the first day accordingly. It can work well to post the syllabus and provide copies.

Know the Drop/Add Policy

Find out about your department's policy for adding students to a class or section. Do you have the authority to add students to an already full class? If students do not come to the first day or two of class, can you (or must you) drop them from the class? How do you drop and add students from the class? How should you handle a wait list?

Organize Yourself

Decide what you're going to wear and make sure it's clean (and ironed if need be!). Pack your bag with everything you will need:

- copies of the course syllabus
- copies of all other handouts
- lesson plan
- class list
- grade book
- pens and pencils
- chalk pens and eraser (if needed)
- index cards for student information
- a watch or a cell phone with a clock

■ **Outfitting Yourself**

What you wear and the accoutrements you bring will affect how you feel about yourself as a teacher and how your students view you.

Teaching Clothes

Unlike many jobs, teaching at a university gives you more flexibility in the formality of your attire. Your clothes should always be clean, well kept, and of appropriate "coverage," but their style is a personal choice.

Dressing Up

PROS   Students can see that you take your job seriously.

You look and may feel more professional.

You may have less trouble establishing your authority in the classroom.

You create a distinction between your teaching job and your student life.

You give your students something nice to look at.

CONS   It creates a greater sense of distance between you and your students (this could also be a pro).

You may not be as comfortable in these clothes.

Nice clothes can be expensive.

Dressing Down

PROS   You may be very comfortable in these clothes.

You probably already own these clothes.

It may make students feel more comfortable approaching you.

CONS   Students may take you less seriously as a teacher.

Students may be more likely to question your authority.

You may feel less "put together."

Outer Wear

If you can leave your coat, hat, umbrella, and so on, in your office before class, do so. It gives you less to keep track of when entering and leaving class. If this is not possible, think about where you want to remove your outdoor gear (in front of the class, in the back of the classroom, in the hall, etc.), especially if it involves pulling a coat over your head.

Bags

Shoulder bags are a popular choice among teaching assistants because they look professional, but a good-looking backpack works as well if you prefer it. You may want to bring the bag to class because it is an easy way to carry papers, pens, and so forth. Unloading your bag in your office, and bringing only the class material you need to the classroom is also an efficient way of organizing yourself before class and making sure that you really do have everything you need.

▨ Introducing Yourself

Many teaching assistants worry that they are ill equipped for teaching if they are barely removed from the undergraduate experience themselves. While you may feel that you have little to offer your students that they cannot offer each other, you will quickly discover that, in fact, you do know much more than they do about your area of study. Remember that your students walk in expecting you to know more than they do, and it is your job on the first day to establish your legitimacy as their teacher.

Your Name

On the first day, you should let your students know what you want to be called; you may want to put your name on the board so that they can see what you want to be called. Many teaching assistants opt to be called by their first name, but using Mr. or Ms. is also a sensible option. To some extent, your decision will affect the formality of your relationship with the students. Do what feels most comfortable for you.

It can be very awkward for students if they do not know how to address you, both in person and in email. Some will default to "Professor _____," which you will have to correct (many undergraduates are not aware of the distinctions among levels of faculty and instructional staff). Others will wait for eye contact to begin speaking rather than addressing you. Others may opt for "Hey!" You can facilitate easier communication from the get-go by establishing how you would like to be addressed.

Your Background

Fundamentally, most of your students assume you are qualified and do not care too much about your official qualifications as a teacher. What they do care about is your interest in and knowledge of the subject you are teaching. The more enthusiastic you are about the course, the more enthusiastic you can expect your students to be. Speak briefly, if at all, about your undergraduate education or experience in your field, but do not belabor this subject (as we said, they don't necessarily care). Some of your previous experiences will also emerge naturally in discussions throughout the term.

There is no reason to discuss your age or the age difference between you and your students unless, for some reason, it becomes relevant. The same is true for other aspects of your personal life; if they see a wedding ring, they will figure out its significance, but outside of that, there is no reason to divulge the details of your personal life, your sexual orientation, and so on, unless you feel this information is relevant to the class.

If they do ask a personal question, you are free to indicate that this question is not relevant, important, or appropriate. You might deal with this humorously ("Actually, I am a very young-looking 89!") or directly ("Right now I am only addressing questions relevant to the course."). Do not worry that you are "blowing the student off." What you are doing is maintaining appropriate student-teacher boundaries and helping students to learn what sorts of questions *are* appropriate for class.

Remember that you can always tell your students more about yourself as the semester progresses, but you cannot take back anything you say on the first day.

Your Gender

Issues of gender are subtle, complex, and extremely powerful, and they are at work in every classroom. When you are thinking about introducing yourself to your students, do not forget that they are also meeting you as their new male or female teacher.

Your gender will influence the power dynamic between you and your students, and it will also influence the power dynamic among your students. While this can be a good thing (e.g., female teachers in the sciences may inspire undergraduate women to consider graduate school), there are an infinite number of ways that the power dynamic in a classroom may be disrupted by issues related to gender.

- Male *and* female students may be less inclined to respect the authority of female teachers.
- Female students may be more or less inclined to speak in a class taught by a man; male students may say more or less in front of female teachers.
- Male students may aim to intimidate female teachers; male teachers may intimidate female students.
- Teachers may be overly flirtatious with their students; students may be overly flirtatious with their teachers.
- Female students may be less respected in some fields (e.g., physics), while male teachers may be less respected in others (e.g., social work).

Regardless of your gender, you should keep in mind that gender dynamics are also at work among the students themselves. Unless you are teaching a class about gender, it is unlikely that you will need or want to make an explicit issue of the gender-related power dynamics in your classroom. However, such issues should be on your mind now and throughout the semester. There are many subtle ways that you can manage gender-related issues in your classroom.

- Be sure that men and women are equal participants in class discussions; if they are not, consider possible reasons for this and make the necessary changes.
- Be nonsexist in your presentation of materials (e.g., using both males and females in your examples).
- Demonstrate that you expect to be respected regardless of your gender by treating all of your students with equal respect.
- While students may come to the class with sexist ideas about male and female teachers, they will almost always respond to a teacher's command of the material, regardless of their gender.

Your Race and Culture

Like issues related to gender, issues related to race and culture are extremely powerful within the classroom. Almost everything noted previously about gender applies to issues of race and culture.

- Students may be less inclined to respect the authority of minority teachers.
- Depending on the teacher's race or culture, minority students or students who are members of the dominant culture may feel less inclined to speak in class.
- Both students and teachers may exploit the power differential that exists among different racial and ethnic groups.
- Regardless of *your* race or culture, race and culture dynamics will be at work among your students.

Additionally, there are some special issues that arise with regard to race and culture.

- While your gender is typically obvious to your students, your race and culture may not be.
- You may not be able to identify your students' racial and cultural backgrounds.
- Racism may result from ignorance—there are many college students who meet people from certain racial or cultural backgrounds for the first time in college; sexism rarely

results from similar ignorance—most college students have had ample contact with competent men and women.

Again, unless you are teaching a course on racial or cultural issues, you may not need or want to make racial and cultural difference an explicit issue in your classroom. As with issues related to gender, the power of racial and cultural differences should be on your mind throughout the semester. You should use your position of authority to make sure that all students are treated respectfully by you and their classmates and that everyone in your classroom has an equal voice. If you suspect that potentially offensive behavior is a result of ignorance, use your role as a teacher to provide students with important information. For example, you might try to catch a student after class or write a note on their paper letting them know that most Native Americans prefer not to be referred to as "Indians."

See pages 57–58 in Chapter 4, Handling Sensitive Material, for more information on addressing sensitive issues in class.

Your Language

Teaching assistants who are non-native English speakers, whether they were born in the United States or abroad, face a different set of challenges in the classroom, sometimes due to real language barriers and sometimes due to student assumptions and/or biases. Students often complain about "foreign TAs" (in non–foreign language classes), and they often judge foreignness by accent.

In most cases, accent differences should not be a problem for you or your students. Indeed, many undergraduates welcome the opportunity to learn from someone from another country. But, you may also discover that some students respond negatively to a foreign accent. At times, some students will transfer their frustration with the material to frustration with your accent. Regardless of the prejudices students have at the beginning of the semester, they will typically respond positively to your competence in and enthusiasm for the field.

You may want to start the term by telling your students where you are from and whatever else about your background you deem appropriate. If you feel that your accent is noticeable, you can acknowledge that and tell your students that they will quickly become accustomed to your speech. Encourage them to ask questions if they ever have trouble understanding what you are saying.

> EXAMPLE   "I know that my accent may be unfamiliar—you
> may have trouble understanding me now, but
> you will become accustomed to my speech after
> a couple of classes. Please feel free to stop me
> and ask (to) me to repeat anything I say that you
> do not understand—it will not be a problem."

At almost all universities, you will have passed an English exam that qualifies you to teach in a U.S. classroom. However, if you find that there is a real language barrier in your classroom, that your students cannot understand your presentation of the material and/or you cannot understand their questions, it is your responsibility to seek help. Contact your university's resource center for international graduate students or seek out published material for international graduate student teachers. Do not feel that a language barrier speaks to your qualifications as a teacher generally; just be sure that you are taking the necessary steps to teach effectively in a predominantly English-speaking classroom.

Establishing Contact

Be clear about how and when students can reach you. Give all this information to students *in writing* on the first day, either on the board or on the syllabus. It's also helpful to put this information on the course management system.

Email

With email, your students can contact you at any hour without interrupting you. You may want to encourage students to use email as a way to ask questions about assignments, make appointments, or even talk about issues that arise in class. Be clear with your students about how often you check email and how promptly they can expect a response.

Email cannot (and should not) replace the one-on-one interaction that is possible during office hours. If a student's questions are too numerous and/or far reaching to be answered appropriately via email, or if you feel the student will learn more from a conversation with you, use your email response to make an appointment with the student to visit you during office hours.

> "It's midnight the night before the paper is due, and the phone rings. Why I answered it, I don't know—I knew it had to be a student. 'I think I lost the assignment sheet,' she said plaintively. 'Can you read it to me so that I can write it down?' That was the last time I gave out my home phone! Email never wakes me up."

Office Phone Number

If your department provides an office where you can be reached or where students can leave messages, give this number to students (with warnings about how quickly the message will get to you).

Home or Cell Phone Number

Giving students your home or cell phone number can be problematic because you may hear from them at inappropriate times and more often than you might wish. If you choose to give students your number, you should give them clear guidelines about when they may call and expect you to answer/respond. Do not expect that they will respect these guidelines. Further, students may see no difference between sending you a text message and sending you an email. But there is a difference. Text messaging is generally for personal communication; your university email account is for professional communication. In general, we do not recommend giving students your home or cell phone number.

Sample Syllabus Heading

Philosophy 234 (Modern German Philosophy), Section 3
MW 1:00–2:30

Joe Schmo, Instructor
Office: K-411 Concrete Hall
Office Phone: 555–4242 (8 AM–5 PM, leave a message with the secretary)
Office Hours: W 2:30–4:00
                          Th 9:00–10:00 (and by appointment)
Email: schmo@univ.edu (I check email M–F 8 AM–6 PM, so this is an easy
           way to ask questions, make an appointment, etc.)

Class Email Groups

To communicate with your class, you may want to set up a class email group. You can use this to send messages to the entire class, and students can use it to get in touch with each other. Many universities also now offer course-based websites (course management systems) where you can post announcements as well as class materials. If you will be sending timely messages through the email group (e.g., assignment updates) or posting them on the website, you must be sure to remind students to check their mail on the website frequently. Set a policy about what constitutes appropriate email to this list (e.g., "no keggers announced here").

Facebook

You may be invited or inclined to "friend" your students on Facebook. There are many reasons not to. One of the greatest challenges facing teaching assistants is maintaining appropriate boundaries between themselves and students, who are often very close in age. Friending students on Facebook can compromise those boundaries. Students have many other ways to communicate with you and do not need to be your Facebook friend. Should a student ask, you can simply state that you have a policy that you don't friend current students. You may choose to friend students after the term. Just remember that the instructor-student relationship does not necessarily end at the end of the term: students may take another course with you or ask for a letter of recommendation.

Whether or not you friend your students or not, don't post anything on Facebook (or any other digital environment) that you would not feel comfortable having your students, colleagues, or prospective employers read. For example, students will have trouble hearing your praise or taking seriously that you enjoy teaching after they have read your post complaining about the tedium of reading their papers. Don't assume that your privacy settings mean that you have full control over who reads your posts.

Office Hours

Most departments require teaching assistants to hold office hours a couple times a week. Try to schedule your hours at a time that is convenient for your students and for you, and be sure to let them know that you can schedule other meeting times if they cannot attend office hours. While it may be tempting to schedule office hours only at your convenience, in the end, you will save yourself time and trouble and, more important, you will be a better teacher by being more readily accessible to your students. That said, schedule office hours in a way that also makes sense with your schedule. If Tuesdays are free, perhaps you don't want to schedule office hours right in the middle of the day. It can work well to schedule office hours adjacent to other commitments you have on campus.

See pages 150–54 in Chapter 8, Office Hours, for more information on holding office hours.

Meeting before and after Class

Students often will expect to be able to grab you after class for a brief consultation, and if that works for your schedule, there is no need to say anything. But if you are on a tight schedule, you should let students know that you will not be available immediately before or after class and that they should plan on arranging a different time to talk to you (office hours, by email, etc.).

▣ Syllabus: Setting the Agenda

Use the syllabus as a kind of contract with your students. It outlines what you expect from your students and what your students can expect in return. As with a legal document, the more specific and detailed you make the policies on the syllabus, the easier they will be to enforce. If you are leading a discussion section for a lecture course, the professor will have provided a syllabus, but you may want to supplement this with your own.

Establishing Policies

Be as detailed as you possibly can with all of your policies about attendance, late work, missed exams, and so on. You will be glad to have these guidelines to follow if/when these issues arise. For example, be specific about how much grades will be lowered for each day an assignment is late or for a missed lab. Part of your job is to establish your authority as a teacher, and having clear policies indicates to your students that you are comfortable in this role.

Setting the Tone for the Semester

The entire syllabus does not have to be seriously worded. You can be amusing but firm about issues like attendance and class participation. Remember that you are letting students get a sense of who you are and how you expect to relate to them. The part on plagiarism, however, should be nothing but serious.

Do not worry about being too strict or sounding too firm about the rules on the first day. As long as your policies are fair, they are beneficial to everyone. Remember that you can always ease up on the rules later in the term, but that it is extremely difficult to become more strict in a way that will seem credible to your students. Students appreciate knowing the rules and the penalties for violating them.

What to Include

The syllabus is the students' reference sheet for the course, so include as much pertinent information as you can. That said, a syllabus should not become novel-like in length or get overly chatty.

Decide what absolutely needs to be on the syllabus and what related explanations can be addressed in class.

Required or Highly Recommended Information
This information should be presented clearly on the syllabus:

- all of your "bureaucratic" information: name, office location and hours, office phone number, email address

- required texts and where to purchase them

- any and all deadlines for assignments and dates for exams

- a breakdown by points or percentages for how much all work and class participation count toward the final grade

- attendance policy: how many absences students are allowed and how further absences will affect a grade (also know the university's policies on religious holidays and students traveling for university-sponsored activities such as athletics—but these may not need to go on the syllabus)

- policy on late work and missed exams

- information about how students with learning disabilities or other special needs can request special accommodations

- the university's policy on plagiarism (it is important to go over this in detail with students, given the usually serious consequences for violating the policy).

> See pages 176–82 in Chapter 8, Plagiarism, for more information on dealing with plagiarism.

Optional Information
Other information may be more appropriate in some classes than others, and much of it can be presented in other forms or forums, rather than on the syllabus itself:

- the course description

- course goals or objectives

- weekly schedule with topics and readings (some instructors provide the schedule in two parts if they have not yet determined what material will need to be covered in the second half of the term)

- brief descriptions of required assignments

- a brief description of what is meant by class participation

- classroom conduct policies: cell phones, laptops, food and drink, email etiquette
- course advice: study tips, note-taking, group work, availability of tutors or other resources
- ways that students can provide you with feedback about the course.

See Appendix A for a sample syllabus.

A Note on Laptops

Many students come to class expecting to use their laptops to take notes and, if they choose to, surf the Internet. There are benefits and drawbacks to laptops in the classroom.

PROS   Many students are very efficient taking notes on a laptop.

Students can access readings or Powerpoint slides online during class.

Students can look up useful and relevant information during class.

CONS Even the most disciplined students have trouble resisting the lure of email, Facebook, and other non–class related Internet activities. Students may claim that they multitask well, but all studies show that divided attention interferes with learning.

Students using laptops for non–class related activities distract the students around them.

Students are looking at their laptops rather than you or their classmates, regardless of what they are doing on their laptops.

You should decide whether students having laptops will be beneficial or detrimental to the learning environment of your classroom and set your policy on laptops accordingly. On the first day, talk explicitly with your students about your policy.

EXAMPLE   "You will see on the syllabus that I have asked you not to use laptops during class. There are a few reasons for this. First, I know firsthand how hard it is not to check email or Facebook or espn.com when you have your laptop in front of you—even when you mean to be paying attention. And studies show that we don't learn as well when our attention is divided. Second, I know you don't intend to distract anyone else when you surf the Internet during class, but the fact is that it is distracting for everyone else who can see your screen—and for me, because I know you're typing when I haven't said anything interesting or noteworthy! Third, when you all are looking at your laptop screens, it keeps us from making eye contact, talking with each other, and learning together. Rest assured that I will give you ample time to take notes by hand, and you can ask me to repeat something at any time. If you find that you can only take notes on a laptop, let me know and we can work out a special arrangement."

◼ The First Class Meeting

The first day of class can set the tone for the term. If you want students to participate during the term, they should participate on the first day.

Do not expect to teach too much content on the first day that your class meets, but try to include some substantive activity. Your main goal is to interest the students in the course and give them a sense of the kinds of issues, questions, and skills the course will address. The other tasks include taking attendance, beginning to learn names, filling out information cards, and going over the syllabus. If you are teaching a science lab, you may use the first day of class to introduce students to the lab and to review safety procedures. We highly recommend not dismissing class early, even though students may come with that expectation. It is a good idea for them to become used to being in class for the full time right from the start. If you think that you won't have enough material to fill all of the class time, consider some of the icebreakers offered later in this chapter (see pages 26–27).

Making Your Entrance

Your students will invariably stop talking and stare at you the moment you enter the classroom. You may find that on the first day you want to arrive right on time because you do not know your students' names and want to avoid this awkward silence. As the semester progresses, you may want to come early to deal with bureaucratic details or to chat with students.

Arriving a Few Minutes Early

PRO   You have time to get organized, arrange chairs, erase the board, talk to students about class assignments, enjoy informal "classroom banter."

CON   You may have to suffer the unbearable silence of sitting with the two or three students who have trickled in early and who will not speak to each other in your presence (and who may feel awkward speaking with you).

Arriving Exactly on Time

PRO   This makes the beginning of class a more clear-cut event (class begins when you arrive), and it avoids the awkwardness of silent dead time before class.

CON   You need to be completely organized before you walk in the door, or you will be forced to start class late. Therefore, you may want to take all of the materials that you will be using during class out of your bag and carry them into the room so that you do not have to unpack your bag while students wait and watch.

Taking Attendance

Write your name and the course name and number on the board so that any students who have suddenly found themselves in the wrong classroom can leave. After you introduce yourself and give as much background as you see fit, you probably will want to go over the class list to see who is and is not there. Be sure to ask students to correct your pronunciation of their name and to tell you if they prefer to be called by something other than their given name. Get the names of any students present in the class who are not on the list, and tell them their status for getting in (or ask to see them after class). Remind all the students of your drop/add policy; for example, they may need to attend the second meeting in order not to be dropped from the class.

In future class sessions, you can take attendance by passing around a sign-up sheet, or you can simply mark who is absent once you know all their names.

"I am compulsively early, and so on the first day of class, I arrived in the classroom ten minutes early. There were three students there who stopped talking when they realized I was the teacher. I had no idea who they were or what to say to them, so we said nothing, which meant that every new student who entered the room became deathly silent when they came in. It was a mean feat to revive that class when those awful ten minutes were finally over."

Learning Names

Learn your students' names as quickly as you can. No excuses allowed here (e.g., "I'm just not good at names"). Focus on it, and you'll be able to do it. You have memorized many more arduous things in your career. It makes an enormous difference with students and the whole class dynamic for you to refer to them by name. Some instructors make notes on their roster to help them remember which students go with which names (e.g., buzz cut, nose ring).

Information Cards

Having a note card with each student's "vital information" can prove invaluable later in the term if you need to get in touch with them. Write on the board (inside a re-creation of a card if you're feeling artistic) all the information you would like them to include. The crucial items: name, phone number, email address. Optional items: their major, interests, expectations of the course, other courses that term, and so forth.

Name:	Year:
Major:	Phone #:
Email:	
Interests in this area:	
Reasons for taking the class:	
Other courses this semester:	

Icebreakers

You may want to try these icebreakers before you go over the syllabus because they can begin to establish a sense of unity in the class. They are a way for you to learn students' names and to get a better sense of the makeup of the class. Also, if you want students to learn each other's names, you must give them a way to meet each other.

Introducing Your Icebreaker

Many students and teaching assistants find any icebreaker to be a painfully corny exercise. They're right. However, icebreakers usually do "break the ice," and students will be more willing to participate in your icebreaker if you acknowledge from the beginning that the task is a corny one while giving your reasons for doing it anyway.

> EXAMPLE "I know that your worst fear about the first day of class is about to be realized, and that exercises like this can seem really silly, but I have found that this is the quickest way for all of us to meet and learn a bit about each other."

Sample Icebreakers
Introducing a Partner

1. Ask students to pair up with someone they do not know. Give each pair a total of four minutes to interview each other. (If you have an odd number of students, one group can include three students.)

2. Tell them that they only need to get basic information such as each other's name, year in college, hometown, and interests. You can also have students find out why their classmates are interested in this course and/or tell each other something particularly memorable about themselves.

3. Watch the time for them, and make sure that they switch roles (from interviewer to interviewee) after two minutes.

4. Give each student about one minute to introduce their partner.

You don't need to participate because you already have introduced yourself. This icebreaker relieves students of the pressure of having to talk about themselves in front of an unfamiliar group, and, by the time you are finished, each student should feel familiar with at least one other person in the class.

Introducing Oneself

Go around the room and ask each student to give their name and year in college. In addition, ask each student to tell the class at least one interesting fact about themselves (or one thing that makes them unique or particularly memorable). You can set the tone of this icebreaker (which can be quite humorous) by going first. For example you might share that you were given an F in singing as a kindergartner or some equally silly tidbit. Or you can ask each student to find a random item in their backpack and explain its significance. As students introduce themselves, you can create a student "map" on the board that you all can use later in the class as you try to remember names. This icebreaker takes less time than the first one, and if you start with some humor, students won't feel too painfully "on the spot."

Reviewing the Syllabus

It is not enough to hand out the syllabus and expect students to read it. They may not. But you don't have to read it to them either. Ask students to read various key paragraphs in the syllabus aloud. Call on one student to read the first key paragraph (this also can be a good way to learn names). After they finish, you can emphasize important points or add any supplemental information (make these notes to yourself beforehand on your syllabus because once you are in class, you may not remember the things that seemed important to you the night before). For the next paragraph, you can either call on another student or ask the first student to choose a classmate to pick up where they left off (this way, they have to start learning each other's names).

You should review your attendance policy, your grading policy, late assignment policy, and the university's rules on plagiarism. The clearer you are about this from the very beginning, the fewer hassles you will run into later (and if these hassles do arise, you have covered yourself).

You do not have to make reviewing the syllabus the first thing you do on the first day of class. You can include a content-based activity on the first day and then go over the syllabus near the end of class.

Using Up Remaining Time

You may want to come prepared with at least one exercise you can use if you have time remaining at the end of class. You can give a brief introductory lecture if you feel comfortable doing so. You also can learn more about the makeup of your class by asking your students an "introductory question."

EXAMPLES "Have you ever felt math anxiety? When?"

"Can people tell where you're from by the way you speak? What do they say?"

"What do you see as your strengths and weaknesses as a writer?"

"Why are you taking this course?"

You can ask students to share their thoughts aloud, either with the full class or in small groups, or you can have them spend five to ten minutes writing in response to the question. You can collect these papers and use them to get a better sense of who your students are and what they know. This material also may work well as an introduction to the next class.

▣ Further Reading

Davis, B. G. 2009. *Tools for Teaching.* 2d ed. San Francisco: Jossey-Bass.

Filene, P. 2005. *The Joy of Teaching: A Practical Guide for New College Instructors.* Chapel Hill: University of North Carolina Press.

Geismar, K., and G. Nicoleau, eds. 1993. *Teaching for Change: Addressing Issues of Difference in the College Classroom.* Cambridge, MA: Harvard Educational Review.

Lie, S. S., and V. O'Leary, eds. 1990. *Storming the Tower: Women in the Academic World.* East Brunswick, NJ: Nichols/GP.

Provitera-McGlynn, A. 2001. *Successful Beginnings for College Teaching: Engaging Your Students from the First Day.* Madison: Atwood Publishing.

Rotenberg, R. 2010. *The Art and Craft of College Teaching: A Guide for New Professors and Graduate Students.* 2d ed. Walnut Creek, CA: Left Coast Press.

Ryan, M. P. 1989. *Planning a College Course: A Guidebook for the Graduate Teaching Assistant.* Ann Arbor, MI: National Center for Research to Improve Postsecondary Teaching and Learning.

Smith, J. 1992. *Communicate: Strategies for International Teaching Assistants.* Englewood Cliffs, NJ: Regents/Prentice Hall.

Svinicki, M., and W.J. McKeachie. 2011. *McKeachie's Teaching Tips: Strategies, Research, and Theory for College and University Teachers.* 13th ed. Belmont, CA: Wadsworth.

Tice, S.L., N. Jackson, L.M. Lambert, and P. Englot, eds. 2005. *University Teaching: A Reference Guide for Graduate Students and Faculty.* 2d ed. Syracuse, NY: Syracuse University Press.

3

Weekly Class Preparation

Even the most experienced teachers need to plan what they will do in every class. This chapter details the steps involved in developing an organized and meaningful lesson plan.

▣ The Goal of the Class

Most teaching assistants meet each week with their class for about one to three hours (labs, of course, are longer). Your job is to use your teaching time to make learning happen. This can occur in many ways. You might impart factual information to your students, help them to clarify and consolidate information that was already presented to them in lecture, encourage them to see old information in new ways, or provide hands-on experience for a concept covered in lecture. Regardless of your approach, your students should know more, understand more, or have something new to think about by the time they pack their bags to head off to their next class.

Setting a Goal

You will be most effective as a teacher if you focus your energies on meeting one or two major goals in a given session. Our first instinct can be to focus purely on the content we hope to cover. We encourage you instead to begin by articulating for yourself what you would say if a colleague stopped you in the hall after class and asked, "What did your students gain from class today?" The answer will be the learning goals that should then drive your decisions about the content you will cover. These goals may be focused on students mastering specific material, grasping broad intellectual questions or approaches that underlie the material, or developing particular analytic skills.

In terms of class content, focus in on the areas that will help you achieve your class goals. Be sure to share with your students the goals behind that day's class content and activities. The key is that students will have an easier time grasping the material if it is clearly related, focused, and contextualized. If they know what it is that they are trying to gain from a particular class, they will be able to gauge their success and ask better questions.

"A lesson plan? You mean I was supposed to have one of those?"

EXAMPLES *Goal:* Help students adopt the appropriate convention for scientific writing by reviewing the proper format for a lab report.

Lesson: Hand out sample lab reports to class; point out the strengths and weaknesses of each. Invite student comments and questions.

Goal: Develop students' capacity to consider controversial issues from multiple perspectives by providing a forum in which students challenge their own ideas about the legalization of marijuana.

Lesson: Organize a debate in which every student is required to argue both sides of the issue.

Goal: Foster the students' understanding of how political climates shape the response to political crises by examining the circumstances surrounding the Bay of Pigs crisis.

Lesson: Assign students to read through the correspondence between Kennedy's advisers before class; divide them into groups at the beginning of class and ask each group to summarize the position of a particular adviser; ask each group to present its summary to the rest of the class; require the entire class to assess the various advisers' points.

Prioritizing Goals

Sometimes you will have a long list of points to cover. In this case, be sure to prioritize your goals and start with the one that is most critical to helping your students understand class material. If you get through the first concept quickly, move on to the next one. Think carefully about how to create a transition between points so that students understand how the material fits together. Always remember that the material is much newer to them than it is to you and that they may not see all the connections as easily as you do.

> "The best analogy I have ever heard about teaching involves books and bookshelves. The concepts in our field are like books. When we teach the concepts, we are giving students books. The key to good teaching is to remember that they may not have a bookshelf on which to put the books. We need to give them books, help them build the bookshelf, and then help them organize the books on the bookshelf."

▨ The Lesson Plan

Once you have established your teaching goal(s) for a particular class, *write it down*. You must be very clear with yourself about what you are trying to teach. Once you have listed your goal(s), sketch a plan to make the relevant concepts accessible and interesting to your students. Before you start writing your lesson plan, make these decisions:

- How much talking will you do, and what will you talk about?
- How much will you expect your students to participate?
- What relevant activities can help you make your point?
- Will your students need to prepare for the class meeting in advance?

If your students will need to do special preparation in advance of your class meeting, be sure to let them know one week ahead of time so that they have fair warning. This means that you will have to be one week ahead of your students in your lesson plans.

Writing a Lesson Plan

Although it may seem silly and tedious, you should carefully plan out everything that you will do in your teaching time by writing it all down. While you may have a very clear plan outlined in your head, it is easy to forget important details once you are faced with the questions and concerns of 20 or more students. This can be especially important in lab classes when reminding students of critical details may make a difference in the outcome of their experiments.

Many teaching assistants use an outline format for their lesson plans. This makes it easier for you to know where you are and where you are headed when you glance at the plan during class. You may even want to color code parts of your lesson plan so that you can find your place quickly once class gets rolling.

Once you have finished your lesson plan, print it out. Reading your class plan from your laptop saves trees, but it can make it hard to teach well. Looking at your screen distances you from your students. Scrolling up and down to find relevant information can be distracting. Reading from a laptop ties you to the desk because you cannot roam around the class with it. And with a laptop you run the risk of experiencing some sort of technology-related problem.

Telling Students the Plan

When you have spent so much time creating your lesson plan, it can be easy to forget that your students come to class with no idea about what you are planning to do. At the beginning of class, give them an overview or brief outline of the plan for the day, including the goals. Classroom activities can work exponentially better when students know how the class time will be spent and understand why they are doing what they are doing.

Facilitating Student Notes

Some students learn and study effectively from well-organized notes, and the organization of their notes depends on your providing structure to the information. If you are lecturing, provide an outline of the major points so that students know where you are going. You can then check them off as you cover them. As you speak, highlight and review the main points so that students can see how they are related and which ideas are subordinate to others.

- Use the board as much as you can. Students know that what you write on the board is important. It also slows you down, which gives students time to take good notes. If you elect to use PowerPoint, be sure to limit the words on each slide and allow students plenty of time to copy slide content.

- Use numbers so that students know how many points you are making and can organize their notes accordingly (e.g., "There are three kinds of insect life in this river. The first . . .").

> See pages 82–88 in Chapter 5, Lecture, for detailed information about giving lectures.

Incorporating Writing

Asking students to write about course material requires them to think through and to fully articulate their ideas. In written assignments, you and your students can get a clearer sense of what they understand and where they are still struggling. Writing can also be an opportunity for students to build an academic argument in a systematic, detailed, and appropriately supported manner. We encourage you to consider incorporating writing assignments in all disciplines, including the natural sciences. By writing, students move immediately from passively receiving information to actively synthesizing ideas and creating original arguments.

Students can often learn more about writing in the course's discipline and about the topic of the paper when given assignments that include submitting a proposal (and getting feedback), writing a draft (and getting feedback), and revising to create the final version of the paper. As you can tell from this description, students need and will benefit from your guidance as they master the expected conventions for a formal paper's content and format within the course's discipline. Students can learn a lot from working through, step by step, the stages involved in getting one paper "right."

Allotting Time

You should guesstimate how long each part of your lesson plan will take and allot your class time so that you will be able to cover all of the necessary material. You can write the number of minutes allowed for each part of the lesson plan or the time at which you expect to begin an activity so that you do not run out of time at the end. Be sure to leave time to wrap up the class and review relevant points. Even though you may have taught with utter clarity and precision, students still will benefit from a brief summary of what just happened in class.

You do not want so strict a lesson plan as to "run over" student questions, but you also do not want to get bogged down in minor issues when major points still desperately need attention. It will help if you have some material near the end of the lesson plan that you see as optional or that you can bump into the next class session. This way you will have the flexibility to dwell longer on a topic that turns out to be of particular interest or concern to students. At the same time, use your judgment and authority to bring closure to a discussion you see as no longer productive or relevant and to steer the students back toward the major topics of the class.

EXAMPLE   "There are so many interesting aspects to this topic, I wish we had time to pursue them all. Let's get back to the core of what we're dealing with today."

Administrative Details

Although administrative matters are not part of your formal lesson for the day, you will want to add them to your lesson plan. This will include things like making plans to talk with individual students, announcing a change in your office hours, scheduling review sessions, or telling students when graded material will be returned to them. This is also a time to solicit student questions about bureaucratic matters that may be relevant to the entire class.

You will usually want to attend to these items before you move into your lesson for the day, and they are likely to be issues that students come to class concerned about. If you wait to cover this at the end of the class, students will have often already shut their notebooks or you will have run out of time. And trust us, write these details down—they will be the first things that you forget once you walk into the classroom.

Lesson Format

Most courses taught by graduate students use one of three (broadly defined) teaching formats: more loosely planned discussion sections, lectures, and more highly structured classes that include pre-planned student activities. Decide on which one you will use for a particular class and then develop your lesson plan accordingly.

Even if the material you are teaching is traditionally presented in a lecture format (and this is how it was presented to you as an undergraduate), do not feel that lecturing is your only option. Almost all lessons can be adapted to a variety of formats; you can transmit a great deal of information while involving your students.

Whatever format you choose for a particular lesson, do not use the same format for every class. Vary your lesson plans from week to week, not only to keep things lively but also to make sure you are reaching students with different learning styles.

Different students learn well in different ways. Some students can take organized lecture notes and absorb the material; others need more active engagement with the material to grasp it. Some students can listen and learn; others are more visually oriented. By mixing up your lesson plans and providing material in different media, you facilitate learning for all students and help them become accustomed to learning material in different ways.

Discussion Classes

If you will be running a discussion, you need to determine your objectives for the discussion. Then think through and write the questions that you will use to get the discussion started. You also need to decide on your role in the discussion: will you be an active participant in the discussion? a facilitator? a devil's advocate if the discussion becomes too lopsided? In addition, decide if students must prepare for the discussion in advance and let them know what they need to do.

See Appendix B for a sample discussion section lesson plan. See Chapter 4 for more information about running a discussion.

Lecture Classes

Though teaching assistants are generally not responsible for lecturing on a regular basis, there may be times when you need to impart a great deal of new information to your students or you need to provide a detailed review of material covered in other parts of the course. At these times, it may be most efficient to give a lecture. Before you give a lecture, be sure to determine precise learning objectives. In other words, what new information and/or skills should your students have by the end of the lecture? Also, let your students know if they should be preparing for the lecture in advance and determine whether you will share an outline of your lecture with your students before class or on the day of the lecture.

See Appendix C for a sample lecture lesson plan.

Structured Student Activities

For highly structured, activity-based classes, you will want to make these decisions before class begins and add them into your lesson plan.

- Will you divide students into groups and, if so, how?

- What instructions will the students need, and how will they get them?

- Will you be writing information on the board? (If so, write out what you will put on the board on your lesson plan so you can just copy it when you get to class.)

- How will you wrap up the lesson?

See Chapter 5 for specific lesson plans for structured student activities.

Time Management

It is fair to expect students to arrive to class on time, but in turn, you must respect their schedules and let them out on time.

Starting on Time

It is critical that you establish the practice of starting class on time. If you wait for the last few students to straggle in, it only encourages tardiness, and students will continue to arrive later and later. It also provides no incentive for typically punctual students to come on time. Once students realize that they will miss important material if they are late, most of them will come on time.

Keeping Time during Class

Prioritize class time. Decide what absolutely must get done that day and give yourself a time cushion, either at the end of an activity or at the end of class. You will probably want to have a watch or clock available, especially if there is no clock in the room or if it is behind you. You may want to put the watch or clock on the table or desk next to you so that you are not constantly looking at your wrist. You have the right to tell students not to start packing up their bags five minutes early, but in exchange, you must end class on time without this or another warning signal from them.

Organizing Space

Keep the physical limitations of your classroom in mind when you are crafting your lesson plans. For example, you will have trouble running an extended full-class discussion if the students' chairs are bolted to the floor in rows. If you feel too limited by the physical realities of your classroom (e.g., it is too small), do not hesitate to seek to be assigned to a more appropriate room.

Arranging Students

If possible, you should arrange the classroom before your students arrive. If not, ask your students to help you. It may seem like a hassle

3: Weekly Class Preparation

to have students pushing chairs around the room, and they may look at you like you're crazy when you tell them to do it, but it will make all the difference in how well a classroom discussion goes. Chair arrangement will depend on class format. In all cases, try to ensure that you can see every student's eyes.

Lecture Oriented

If you will be spending most of the time "imparting knowledge" to your wide-eyed students, every student should be able to see you and the board and have a place to write. This usually requires a more traditional students-facing-teacher classroom setup.

Discussion Oriented

If you are trying to encourage students to talk with each other about the material, no one should be looking at anyone else's back. A circle is usually the best arrangement—and make it a good circle. Students naturally create lackadaisical circles, with some students only half in and some students centered. Take the reins and force them to practice their geometric skills in creating a fairly round, well-balanced circle. Lopsided circles almost invariably lead to poorly balanced discussions.

Lecture and Discussion Oriented

If you are starting with a lecture and then moving into a full-class discussion, wait until it is time for the discussion to ask students to arrange their desks or chairs in a circle. You then can use the movement of everyone into a circle as an obvious signal that full-class discussion is about to begin (and it's always a good way to make sure that everyone is awake!). Or you can put students in a semicircle for the entire class, such that they can see the board and talk with each other.

Placing Yourself

Again, where you put yourself in the classroom depends on the kind of teaching you are doing.

Lecture Oriented

Naturally this places you in the front of the classroom. You can lessen the distance between you and your students by moving tables, podiums, and so on, out of the way if they stand between you and the students. In order to keep your students awake and interested, you may want to move around the front of the classroom (a good reason to move large, sharp-cornered furniture) or even around the entire classroom.

Discussion Oriented

Once you have created a near-perfect circle, place yourself as part of that circle. You may want to keep yourself near the board if you will need to use it.

Lecture and Discussion Oriented

If you are doing a combination of lecture and discussion, you may want to arrange the chairs in a semicircle with you in the front. When you are lecturing, you should stand, especially if you need to use the board. When you join the class in discussion, you should sit (behind a front table, at a chair, on the table, etc.). Remember that how you place yourself, whether you stand or sit, affects how students will interact with you and the material that you are presenting at that moment.

Interacting with the Professor

If you are leading a discussion section for a larger lecture course, your relationship with the professor can be easy, treacherously tricky, or anywhere in between. The professor may or may not explicitly set guidelines for your section—both situations can be problematic or productive. There are some basic guidelines that both you and the professor should follow.

Feedback to the Professor

Because of your close interaction with the students and their work, you have access to information about the course and the students that the professor may not. It is your responsibility to tell the professor certain information about students, such as:

- a concept the professor covered in lecture that confused students and requires review

- a section of an exam on which many students did poorly

- consistent problems students are having with writing assignments or their writing

- a student who is causing problems or who is consistently not coming to class

- a student who is consistently complaining about grades.

Feedback from the Professor

The amount of help and guidance that professors offer to their teaching assistants varies, but there are many ways that professors can make your life easier if they are willing. You should not hesitate to ask for any of the following, even if they are not offered:

- an outline or other guidance on information the professor would like covered in the class

- clarification of attendance or late work policies

- a meeting with you about what material will be covered on the exam

- a meeting to go over an exam, its answers, and a grading policy

- a few graded papers for the first assignment so that you can get a sense of the professor's expectations and grading range.

Your Public Relationship with the Professor

No matter what your personal feelings about the professor and their teaching style, you must keep your public relationship with them professional and maintain a "united front." You should not criticize the professor in front of your students, even if they are complaining, and you should not question the professor's abilities as a scholar or a teacher. You may use your class as a time to present alternate viewpoints or additional information, but you also are responsible for helping the students understand the material the professor presents in class, so you may not dismiss it.

After a lecture with which you do not agree:

DON'T "Don't pay attention to what Professor Engels was saying in class yesterday. He is a Marxist, and he still believes in that outdated theory; he doesn't seem interested in recent scholarship, so I'll have to fill you in."

DO "There are many schools of thought and interpretation when it comes to a question like this one. Professor Engels is presenting a Marxist position. Let's make sure that you understand the elements involved in this interpretation and its strengths and weaknesses. Then if you're interested, I can explain some of the alternative interpretations."

After a student complains to you about the professor:

DON'T "I understand what you're saying. Professor Leslie can be dismissive and isn't always good about answering questions. Other students have had trouble in the past. And she isn't very good about answering my questions either."

DO "I know that Professor Leslie can be intimidating sometimes, but she is very knowledgeable, and you should feel free to go to her office hours with questions. You are also always welcome to talk to me about material you don't understand—we both are here as resources for you."

Remember that some day soon you too may be a professor teaching a course with teaching assistants; think about how you would want these graduate students to treat you and the material that you present in lecture and act accordingly.

Addressing Problems

Every class comes with its own unique challenges. Having difficulties with a class, or in your dealings with an individual student, is a normal and expected part of teaching. Throughout the remainder of this book, you'll find guidance on addressing some of the most common problems that college teachers face. In general, we encourage you to insert an important step between recognizing and responding to problems. We call this step "diagnosing the problem" and have found that taking the time to understand the root cause of a problem goes a long way toward fixing it.

Making a Diagnosis

Once you have identified a problem in your class, you'll want to investigate its cause before deciding on a solution.

> EXAMPLE   One student arrives to class late every day.

> DON'T   Develop an ad hoc lateness policy; lock the class-room door once class begins; humiliate the student in front of their peers.

> DO   Find time to catch the student after class and ask why they are coming to class late.

Using a Diagnosis to Find a Solution

Once you understand the reasons behind a particular problem, you and the student(s) will be able to come up with the most appropriate solution.

> EXAMPLE   The student is consistently late because the class that they have before yours is on the far side of campus, making a timely arrival to your class impossible. You and the student can discuss ways to diminish the disruption of the student's late arrival.

The student complains that the class is too early. You remind the student that they knew the class time when they enrolled and that the lateness policy applies to early birds and night owls alike.

It is often the case that taking the time to diagnose the problem fixes the problem. For example, few students will continue to come to class late once an instructor has inquired about their lateness.

Further Reading

Bain, K. 2004. *What the Best College Teachers Do.* Cambridge, MA: Harvard University Press.

Bligh, D. A. 2000. *What's the Use of Lectures?* San Francisco: Jossey-Bass.

Cannon, R., and D. Newble. 2000. *A Handbook for Teachers in Universities and Colleges: A Guide to Improving Teaching Methods.* 4th ed. London: Kogan Page.

Davis, B. G. 2009. *Tools for Teaching.* 2d. ed. San Francisco: Jossey-Bass.

Fink, L. D. 2003. *Creating Significant Learning Experiences: An Integrated Approach to Designing College Courses.* San Francisco: Jossey-Bass.

Leamnson, R. 1999. *Thinking about Teaching and Learning: Developing Habits of Learning with First Year College and University Students.* Sterling, VA: Stylus; Oakhill, Eng.: Trentham Books.

Lowman, J. 1995. *Mastering the Techniques of Teaching.* 2d ed. San Francisco: Jossey-Bass.

Meagher, L. D., and T. G. Devine. 1993. *Handbook on College Teaching.* Durango, CO: Hollowbrook.

Svinicki, M., and W. J. McKeachie. 2011. *McKeachie's Teaching Tips: Strategies, Research, and Theory for College and University Teachers.* 13th ed. Belmont, CA: Wadsworth.

Running a Discussion

Running a good discussion is like writing a good essay: you need a strong opening, a well-organized body, and a coherent ending. Most of this chapter is relevant only to teaching assistants leading discussion sections or teaching introductory (probably non-science) courses. However, these tips will be helpful to anyone running a discussion-oriented class.

■ Discussions versus Task-Based Participation

Just because sections are often called "discussion sections" does not mean that all the student participation in your classroom will be actual discussion. (It seems more obvious that at universities that call sections "recitation sections," neither you nor the students are spending the whole time reciting.) It is useful to distinguish between two different kinds of student participation: discussion and task-based participation. Both can be very productive learning experiences, and the decision about which to use will depend on your goals for any given class.

In a discussion, you begin with real questions to which you do not have a definitive answer, and you are open to and interested in your students' responses. You do not have an agenda about exactly what material needs to be covered and how. In other words, your goal for the discussion focuses on having the students think with you about an issue rather than covering predetermined content in a particular sequence.

Sometimes you do have an agenda for what specific material needs to be covered, and you want students to participate in the process of covering that material. Obviously, this is not a "genuine discussion" because you know where you are headed—and your students know you have a destination in mind. But it can be a better learning experience for students to participate rather than simply listen to you lecture. The deadliest "discussions" happen when an instructor frames what is a task-based activity as real, open discussion.

As you prepare your lesson plan, you want to be clear with yourself about whether your class will be a discussion or task-based participation (or both). You will then be able to be clear with your students about what you have planned and why.

▣ Arranging the Classroom

The physical arrangement of the classroom will influence the quality of your discussion. Students who are sitting where they cannot be seen by you or their classmates may not feel expected or encouraged to participate in the discussion. We recommend that you help your students to create a well-formed circle.

See pages 38–40 in Chapter 3, Organizing Space, for more information on organizing classroom space.

▣ Initiating Student Participation

Use your discussion opening to inform students of the topic you have in mind for class and of your expectations for the day's activities. Remember that you already have spent a great deal of time planning the class; students, however, arrive with no idea of what you have in mind. Your opening orients your students to how your class plan fits within the broader goals of the course. Several ways to introduce your topic and generate student participation are detailed here.

Make a List

You can ask a question to the class and generate a list of responses on the board, or you can ask each student to share one idea or item off the top of their head. (If you are not using the board for such an activity, jot down notes to yourself on a piece of paper as students talk.) You then have material with which to begin.

EXAMPLE   *Discussion:* "Let's make two lists here on the board of all the pros and cons you can think of for the use of politically correct language."

Task-based participation: "The author of the article uses at least four different kinds of evidence to support her argument. When you write your papers, you will also be drawing on these kinds of evidence. So take five minutes in pairs to identify all the different kinds of evidence you can, and then we'll go over them together."

Freewriting

Freewriting can help students to formulate their ideas before participating in a full-class activity. Ask all the students to get out a piece of paper; give them a question and five or ten minutes to answer it. Tell them you will not be collecting the paper; you just want to see their pens moving the full five or ten minutes. Once they have done this, every student has *something* to say, and you can move into your activity from there. After the time for freewriting has ended, you can call on students—or ask students to volunteer—to read part of what they have written.

EXAMPLE   *Discussion:* "Take out a piece of paper—I'm going to ask you to write continuously for six minutes. On Monday in lecture we watched a documentary about endangered species in Alaska. Take this time to write about your reactions to the film, whatever they were: questions you had, emotions you felt, whatever comes to mind."

> *Task-based participation:* "Get out a piece of paper—you are not going to have to turn this in. Take the next five minutes and write down as much as you can remember from yesterday's explanation in lecture of DNA coding. Then we can work together on filling in any holes."

Pair and Share

This tried-and-true teaching strategy is a terrific way to get students talking to each other and then moving into a full-class activity. Put students into pairs and give each pair a task or question. Depending on your lesson plan, you may want to give different tasks to each pair or give them all the same question. Make the goal clear: for example, as a pair they will tell their classmates about their thoughts on a particular issue; they will share two ideas with the class; they should write a paragraph that they then will give to another pair; and so forth. Pair time allows shyer students to check out their ideas with one other person before sharing them with the group, and it gives all the students a very informal "warm-up" time before a fuller class discussion.

> EXAMPLE   *Discussion:* "Find a partner. Together, make a decision about which two diagnoses might be removed or dramatically changed in the next edition of the psychiatric diagnostic manual. Be sure to have a justification for your choices."
>
> *Task-based participation:* "Choose a partner and together take five minutes to come up with four examples of 'abnormal' behavior that are situationally dependent. At the end of five minutes, I will go around the room and ask you to share your responses with the rest of the class."

Small Group Activities

Small group activities follow the same format as Pair and Share; give groups a question or task and make the goal clear. Then, ask each group to integrate its work into a full-class activity. Figure out ahead of time how you are going to make the groups. You can form groups by where students are sitting, which allows friends to talk comfortably with friends but which can also (a) lead to some discussion unrelated to the course and (b) prevent students from meeting other students in the class. You can "number off" around the room and have all the "ones" work together, and so on. You can make groups ahead of time if you want to ensure that you have at least one good talker in each group.

> See page 71 in Chapter 5, Grouping Strategies, for more information on putting students into working groups.

Read a Passage from the Text

If you want to talk about a text in class, you can "warm up" by reading and discussing one passage from the text. Reasons to use this strategy:

- It gives students a foothold for discussing the entire text.
- It reminds students what the text is about (remember that students may well have done work for other classes since the time they read this text).
- If some students have not read the entire text, it still engages them in the planned activity for the day.

Pick a passage that highlights whatever theme(s) you want to address first and ask a student to read it aloud. Then, have a series of follow-up questions prepared. If you are trying to encourage students to do close reading, use this as an opportunity to dive into the details of the passage.

> See Appendix D for an annotated passage with several possible follow-up questions.

Encouraging Active Student Reading

You should give your students tips about how they can prepare readings before they come to class. Specifically, college students should be urged to read with a pen or pencil in hand. Help your students see the utility of marking noteworthy passages and annotating a text as they read. The most effective way to do this is to have them mark up passages during class so that they get used to the idea of writing in their books and see how this can help them do close readings and process the material.

> EXAMPLE   *Task-based participation:* Ask students to mark all
> the passive constructions in a lab write-up and
> then talk about how the use of passive con-
> structions affects the tone of the writing.

You also can give students this type of assignment ahead of time, so that they have something to look for while they do the reading.

> EXAMPLE   *Discussion:* "As you're reading, mark all the pas-
> sages where you think the material is extrane-
> ous—in other words, you don't see why it's
> there. Then together we'll be able to see if you
> all agree and talk about why the author may
> have included this material in the novel."

Ask a Question

The right question to the full class (which is, of course, sitting in a perfect circle) can get a good discussion rolling. See the following section for tips on quality questioning.

See Chapter 5 for specific structured class plans that end with a discussion.

Effective Discussion Questions

Good discussions require effective questions. Asking good discussion questions is a skill that takes experience and preparation. You cannot walk into class and generate a meaningful discussion by asking questions off the top of your head. Instructors who begin by asking, "So what did you think of the reading?" are almost always greeted with painful silence. Students respond well to questions that are specific and interesting, questions that invite original contributions. Students do not respond well to broad, basic, or "fake" questions. In general, focus on asking "how" and "why" questions rather than "what" and "who" questions.

Asking the First Questions

Write out a series of discussion questions as you prepare the lesson plans for the class. These questions should be directly related to your goal(s) for that class. They should be questions that interest you and will interest your students. Be prepared to think up more questions as you go, but it is a nice safety net to have a few written questions beforehand. Also be prepared to play devil's advocate, to challenge students' views if no one else will.

You may choose to start with a big question that will (you hope!) generate sustained discussion. You may also choose to start with smaller, more discrete questions that can build toward a more substantial question connected to your goal(s) for the class.

Overbroad Questions

DON'T "What did you think of the reading?"

DO   "If you were a dialect speaker from Tennessee, how do you think you would feel about the author's description of your dialect?"

"Talking Down" Questions

DON'T "Who is the author?"

DO   "Could you tell anything about the author's background from the article?" (Be prepared to tell them about the author if you are going to ask a question like this.)

"Read my Mind" Questions

DON'T "Why is human cloning unethical?"

DO "Imagine you sit on this university's ethics panel, and a professor wants to start a human cloning program. What questions would you want to have answered and why?"

Questions with Right and Wrong Answers

DON'T "What is the author's point in this essay?"

DO "Let's read the first paragraph together. . . . Did it make you want to keep reading? Why or why not?"

"Testing for Reading" Questions

DON'T "What three facts does the author use to support her contention that teaching assistants should be worshiped?"

DO (If necessary) "How many of you finished the reading for today? What happened? What are we going to do about this?"

You will notice that some of the Don't examples for discussion questions could legitimately introduce a task-based activity (see page 45). It helps students when you do not confuse discussions and task-based participation.

Why Students May Not Talk

At times, you may ask the most compelling questions imaginable and still be met with cold silence from your students. Here are a few causes of and solutions to the silent-student syndrome.

Peer Pressure

Peer pressure is at work in every classroom, and students usually are as (or more) concerned with what their peers think of them as they are with what you think of them. They do not want to say something stupid, and they do not want to look like a teacher's pet. So you will do better asking questions that solicit opinions rather than right/wrong answers because students run less risk of "losing face" with these kinds of answers.

Time to Think

One of the most painful parts of starting a discussion can be the silence. Get used to it. You thought up the question before class, but the students are hearing it for the first time, and they need a minute or two to think about it. Let the silence hang there for longer than you think you can bear (make yourself count to 20 slowly); generally a student will finally step in to fill the void and start the discussion. If you know that you are asking a tough question, tell the class that you will give them some time to think before soliciting answers. This way, the silence is planned rather than awkward.

Very Difficult Material

Even when students are prepared for class, they may not participate if they feel overwhelmed by the difficulty of the material. Sharing with them that you find parts of the material difficult can authorize them to speak about the material as well. It does not diminish your authority to acknowledge that material is difficult. You can say something like: "This a very challenging reading. I know that I am feeling confused by the first paragraph on p. 12. Why don't we start here—I am hoping some of you have insights about what this means. Then we can look at places where you felt stumped."

Lack of Preparation

If no student steps up to break the silence and you cannot bear it any longer, do not ask an easier question: "Okay, who is the author?" Why should any student stoop to answer this question? If you are trying to determine whether or not students did the reading, ask them. They will be surprisingly (often brutally) honest with you.

Class Dynamics

Depending on the makeup of the class, you may find that some students do not feel comfortable volunteering to participate. You need to be particularly aware of the willingness of female students and students that represent a minority voice in the classroom to take part in full-class discussions. Be conscious of how often you call on and in other ways involve students of different genders, races, and ages, and work to facilitate the participation of the students who seem more reticent to volunteer their opinions in this setting.

Quiet Students

Some very eager and interested students do not feel comfortable participating in full-class discussions. Be sympathetic and be careful about putting these students on the spot.

Outside Forces

There are times during the term (e.g., midterms, fraternity and sorority rush) when students tend to be tired or stressed or overly busy or distracted.

See pages 59–60 in this chapter, Quiet Students, for more information on how to handle quiet students.

They drag themselves to class, but their presence is merely physical. If you try to start a discussion on one of these days and you find that you are facing exhaustion-induced silence, try stepping back and asking the students directly, and empathetically, what is going on (an activity we call "meta-teaching"). They will appreciate your recognition that they have concerns outside your class. And, more important, it will start students talking. You then can guide the conversation toward the lesson you have planned.

See pages 200–2 in Chapter 9, Meta-Teaching, for more details on talking to your students about the class.

Facilitating Discussion

One of the most important elements of a successful classroom discussion is a good balance of voices, including your own.

Your Role as the Teacher

Navigating your role in a full-class discussion is one of the most difficult parts of learning to teach. Do not become frustrated with yourself if you are feeling less than stellar in this area; it can and will take years to get comfortable as a discussion leader.

The crucial element is to think of yourself as a facilitator: you are helping the students talk about a particular topic, and what they say may or may not surprise you. Be prepared to let the discussion follow its natural course as long as it is not moving too far away from your goals for the class. As long as the discussion is germane to the topic, it is most important that students are talking about issues that *they* find intriguing. You do not have to know all the answers along the way, and you should feel free to look to them for their expertise. You will find that they often will be able to answer each other's questions; and they can find it empowering to be able to do so.

As a discussion facilitator, you should keep in mind some overarching goals.

Help students participate.

DON'T   Embarrass a student for any comment. You never want a student to be sorry they spoke.

Do   Take all comments seriously, and help students find what is most important, interesting, or accurate in what they are saying.

Regularly provide positive feedback to students for their contributions (e.g., "Great question" or "You know, I never thought about that before").

Encourage equal participation by students of different genders, races, and ages.

Help students speak and respond to each other.

DON'T   Respond to every student comment yourself. Students may then speak only to you, and discussions may become stilted as students wait for your intervention after each comment.

Do   Encourage student responses: "How do the rest of you feel about Harriet's comment that no one version of a country's history is better than another?"

Encourage students to respond to each other directly (without raising hands, if possible). Step in to summarize or redirect the discussion when necessary.

Help students explore a variety of viewpoints.

DON'T   Weigh in with your own opinion too quickly. Students are often looking for "canned" or simple answers to difficult questions, and they may adopt your opinion as "truth."

Do   Solicit a variety of opinions; ask students to come
       up with counterpoints to their own and each other's
       arguments.

Help keep discussion moving.

DON'T   Let the discussion get stuck because an interesting
         topic has been exhausted.

Do   Summarize the content of the discussion when it is
       beginning to wind down. Help students consider a
       fresh but related topic.

Help keep the discussion on track.

DON'T   Let students stray too far from your goals for the
         class.

Do   Step in when you sense a serious detour. Explain
       that while this is an interesting line of thought, it
       will take you too far afield.

Help students see gaps in their understanding.

DON'T   Tell students that they are wrong or that they missed
         the point.

Do   Acknowledge that this is a confusing issue or prob-
       lem, gently correct the misunderstanding or error,
       and point out where the student is on the right
       track.

Help students see connections and the bigger picture.

DON'T   Let the discussion jump freely from topic to topic.

Do   Tie together various students' comments on one
       topic, explicitly stating connections (e.g., "Karen, your
       question brings us back to Jared's earlier comment").

       Summarize points and counterpoints or dilemmas
       with which students are struggling. Taking notes on
       students' comments as the discussion progresses will
       help.

▣ Handling Sensitive Material

At times, your course may call for the discussion of a sensitive topic. Questions involving issues of gender, race, culture, class, sexual orientation, or any other "political" topic will make the task of running a free-flowing, balanced, and thoughtful discussion more challenging than usual.

Lay Some Ground Rules

Acknowledge from the outset that you are discussing a sensitive topic. Make it clear to your students that you expect them to treat each other with respect. Encourage them to be respectful of each other's opinions and to question the quality of the arguments offered, not the validity of each other's personal beliefs.

EXAMPLE "Over the weekend you read about the debate over affirmative action. I suspect that this is an area where many of you have strong personal feelings. The fact that this is a sensitive topic makes it all the more important that we are able to discuss it in a forum like this. We want to explore all sides of this issue, so don't feel that the points you raise have to match your personal beliefs. By the same token, we must remember that we are evaluating arguments, not the people who raise them. This is going to be a very challenging issue to discuss, but I think that we can do it well. I know that you all can deal with this topic and each other in a sensitive way."

Create a Safe Space

Ask your students to listen to each other and not to judge anyone else too quickly. If they disagree, they should speak up to try to show their classmate(s) where they think they are wrong. Stewing in silent indignation is not fair and does not help others learn.

Tell Students to Beware of "Us" and "Them"

Remind your students they cannot tell much by looking at each other. In many cases, they will not know if one of their classmates is HIV positive, a member of a racial or religious minority, a communist, a welfare recipient, or anything else unless that classmate chooses to volunteer the information. Students should discuss the topic at hand with these possibilities in mind.

Question Carefully

You can encourage students to think about material in a thoughtful (as opposed to reactive) way by directing their thinking with your questions. It often helps to start the discussion in an "objective" way, asking about what arguments exist on either side of an issue or what relevant ideas students have heard. In this way, you are not directly soliciting students' personal opinions, thus creating a safer space.

> EXAMPLE   "What political influences tend to bring about welfare reforms? What ulterior motives for these reforms exist on both sides of the congressional aisle?"

See pages 75–76 in Chapter 5, Debate/Pros and Cons, for specific class plans that work well for handling sensitive or controversial issues.

Be the Devil's Advocate

Discussions of sensitive material can become lopsided for any number of reasons. Students may be hesitant to say anything that does not sound politically correct, a variety of views may not be present in the classroom, or students may feel reluctant to challenge each other's thinking. If the discussion is not well rounded, you need to offer the underrepresented position, regardless of your personal feelings on the matter.

> EXAMPLE   "But one could argue (and people do) that people on welfare don't want to work. What evidence possibly supports this argument?"

▣ Handling Discussion-Stopping Students

At times, students will behave in a way that can potentially stifle even the most promising discussion. This can happen because the students are misbehaving or not doing anything at all. Never allow yourself to become visibly angry with them or with the entire class. Expressing anger with students is a no-win situation for you. It displays a loss of control and professional demeanor, which is more likely to exacerbate the students' behavior than improve it. Instead, try these techniques.

Quiet Students

In every class, there will be quieter students who do not feel as (or at all) comfortable participating in a full-class discussion. One of the benefits of the Pair and Share activity or small group activities is that they provide these students with more of a voice. Once you have identified who these students are, you should think carefully about when you want to call on them in class. Make eye contact with them during a discussion to see if they might want to voice an opinion.

DON'T   Put quiet students on the spot by calling on them in a full-class discussion—it will only make speaking in class more frightening.

DO   Call on quiet students after a freewriting exercise when you know that they have something already prepared or after they have been discussing an issue in a pair.

Do not hesitate to say something to these quieter students in a one-on-one setting. If one of these students spoke up in class, you can reinforce their participation by writing about it in an email or in your comments on a returned paper.

EXAMPLE   "Thanks for making your classmates reconsider their opinions by asking about the consequences of banning cigarettes. I hope we'll continue to hear your voice in class—you have lots of good things to contribute."

You also can remind students in a midterm conference that participation is part of their final grade and that if they do not feel comfortable talking in a full-class setting, you need to see them making a real effort in small groups or talking to you on email or during office hours. There are many ways to participate.

Disruptive Students

Disruptive students are not necessarily loud and obnoxious. Rather, they are students who choose, often in subtle ways, not to participate in the class or who encourage other students not to participate. They are often the students who look or act like they do not want to be in your class.

Do not teach to disruptive students. They are the squeaky wheels, and you will often find yourself bending over backward to please them or get them interested in class.

DON'T   Screw up a good discussion by trying to force a recalcitrant student to participate.

DO   Keep your radar focused on all the students and recognize that there may be some students who are not going to immerse themselves in the classroom activities.

The other students are aware of the disruptive students' behavior, and they too are often happy to let these nonparticipants sit on the sidelines. Here are some disruptive student Hall of Famers and some suggestions for what you can do.

The Newspaper Reader

Class is rolling, and a student is still reading the newspaper. The most effective remedy to this situation is the direct approach: "Joe, this is not the time to read the paper. You can do that after class." It does not hurt to show students that you do not tolerate blatant displays of inattention, and very few students will continue to read a newspaper after being directly told not to do so.

The Texter

This student keeps pulling their phone out of their pocket and texting under the desk, clearly believing that if the phone is under the desk, you can't possibly be aware of what they're doing. As with the newspaper reader, directly ask the student to please save texting for after class. Some instructors establish with students on the first day a policy of what will happen if they get caught texting in class. Consequences can include the student being asked to put the phone away, the class being counted as an absence for the student, and/or the instructor texting the student's friend to let them know the student can't text right now because they are in class.

The Off-Task Laptop User

You are telling an anecdote to the class, and this student is typing away. It is completely clear to you that this student is doing something non–class related on their laptop. If you are a roaming instructor, walk toward the student—that should take care of it. After class, consider pulling the student aside and asking if they need the laptop to take notes in your course. If they say yes, point out that they seem to be distracted at times by the laptop; add that you trust this will not be a problem going forward.

The Whisperers

You are talking to the class or a student is speaking, and there are two students whispering to each other about clearly non–class-related things. You can try the direct approach of asking them to stop talking when others are talking (you can interrupt your own monologue or wait until the other student is finished speaking). You might say something like, "When you guys are talking it makes it hard for the rest of us to hear each other; please save it for after class." You also can walk over to stand near them if you are lecturing (and you are a roving lecturer). Or you can halt the discussion and wait until they notice that their whispers are the only noise in the room. At times, students do whisper to each other about class-related ideas. You can feel free to give students the benefit of the doubt and (kindly) ask them to share their thoughts with the class. This approach engages interested students and stops non-class chitchat.

The Discussion Hog

Every time you ask a question or ask for a volunteer, this student's hand shoots up or they just begin talking. Very often these students have the best intentions and are friendly, outgoing people; but they are still unfairly monopolizing full-class discussion and your attention. A direct and gentle approach usually works well with these students.

> EXAMPLE   "Sylvia, I'll come back to you shortly; let's see if someone else wants to grab the floor for a minute."

If the student persists in monopolizing class time after a few class meetings where you have tried to manage their behavior during class, arrange to meet with the student individually. Reinforce for them that you appreciate their participation in the class but remind them of their responsibility to let others speak.

The Antagonistic Debater

This student verbally challenges you or other students on a regular basis. Perhaps they feel that you are too liberal or too conservative in your views, or perhaps they simply enjoy disagreeing with you to see if you'll get flustered. You must put up with a healthy amount of disagreement in the classroom. You want to encourage students to question their classmates' and their teachers' statements as they would any others. But you also have the right to expect these challenging remarks to be phrased appropriately. When the student verbalizes a contradictory opinion, feel free to ask follow-up questions and force them to articulate their ideas. And be sure to answer antagonistic remarks with thoughtful consideration; in this way, you move the discussion out of empty rhetoric and back into intellectual discourse.

> EXAMPLES   "Why is Darwin's theory of evolution 'stupid'? (Is 'stupid' really the best description, Irene?) What problems does it present, and what do you see as the alternatives?"
>
> "Joe, you say that you think this article is ridiculously biased. How do you think the author could strengthen her argument?"

The Bomb Dropper

Occasionally, you will come across students who use explosive language to express their ideas. Few teachers forget the first time a student makes a comment so offensive that the entire class comes to a halt. Managing this classroom event is a challenge for even the most seasoned instructor. Once you get your jaw off the floor you must do your best to turn the student's comment into a teachable moment.

EXAMPLES "Steven has proposed that women who are raped want sex but are afraid to ask for it. The tension created by his comment is palpable. Why does his statement cause such an emotional response? Can we pause for a moment and think through how his idea could be engaged in an academic, not a polemical, manner?"

"Mary suggests that white people should be allowed to use the 'n-word' freely given that many African Americans now do so. Would the feeling in the room be different right now if Mary had not elected to use the actual word in making her comment? Why? Mary's idea is an interesting one; can someone raise the same question in a way that gets a fruitful discussion going?"

As the course instructor, your job is to model how scholars engage with difficult or sensitive material in academically productive ways.

The Silent Glarer

Every class meeting, no matter what you are doing or saying, this student is sitting in their chair, arms folded, glaring at you to let you know that they are not going to participate in—let alone enjoy—your class under any circumstances. At times, this student may take a break from their glaring to mutter obviously derogatory comments about you and/or the class to their neighbor. For the first one or two class meetings, try to involve this student as best you can while being fair to the other students: call on them as you would a quiet student or try to put them in a talkative small group. If these efforts don't succeed, you must waste no time in reaching out to this student. Do not give in to the temptation to ignore the student's silent protest. Their attitude is deadly to class morale, and their immature behavior can often be addressed effectively with a mature response.

Catch the student after class or send them an email to let them know that you are aware that the course is not working well for them and to invite them to identify their concerns. With substantive feedback, you will have a basis for working with the student to solve the problem. Even if the student ignores your overture, most silent glarers will be better behaved in class once they've been approached directly.

> "After teaching a class in which I had ignored a silent glarer for the entire semester, I happened to be enrolled in a class where one of the other students alternated between silent glaring and quiet complaining about the (very competent) instructor! As a fellow student, I was incredibly distracted by 'who's-with-me-in-thinking-this-teacher-sucks?' dynamic created by the student. I was desperate for the instructor to intervene. It made me realize that I should have said something to my own silent glarer."

EXAMPLE   "Jonas, I'm sensing that you have some concerns about the class. It would be useful for me to know what they are to see if there's anything we can do."

Wrapping Up a Discussion

Think of a class as a well-written essay or article. The last paragraph(s) should remind the reader of the question they are to consider or the point they are to remember. It may sound rehearsed to think of your closing statements ahead of time, but the best instructors have as solid an ending as a beginning to their lectures or discussions. If you start the class with a list or story, perhaps you want to return to that. If you start with a passage from the text, perhaps you want to return to that or another passage from the text to finish. You can always return to your goals for the class and remind students why you all did what you did.

Do not end class purely by time.

> DON'T   Oh my gosh, I guess that's the end of our time. We'll finish up this discussion at the beginning of the next class. Think about what we've discussed!"
>
> DO   Leave yourself enough time to summarize what was discussed, to tie things up, and to provide students with a sense of what they have accomplished that day.

Do not feel you have to give the answer.

> DON'T   "The price we have paid for technological advances is too high. My research focuses on what we've done to the environment, and we cannot possibly justify it."
>
> DO   "You've all expressed some very contradictory opinions that show how difficult the question is. There are valid arguments on both sides, and smart people disagree on this issue. The fundamental problem is that it comes down to how we feel about the importance of technology and what we're willing to sacrifice for progress on this front. Next week, we'll be talking about water pollution, which will raise many of the same issues, so keep this discussion in mind while you're doing the reading this week."

Try to relate this class to those before and after it, as well as to the course goals.

Students benefit if they can understand the progression of the course, how last week's discussion relates to this week's debate. In your role as class guide, help students see the progression of the course. They will be better able to engage and discuss specific course material when they know how the material fits into the broader context of the course.

EXAMPLES "Today we have been talking about whether an anthropologist can ever claim to understand another culture. Is observation sufficient for understanding? When you read the article for this week, keep this question in mind as you read about John Gaze's methodology. Does he have sufficient evidence to make his claims? We'll start with this issue next time."

"Last week you all raised the question of whether Shakespeare's poetry was ever written to be read or only to be heard and how that might change the way in which we analyze the sonnets. Today we've been looking at poems clearly meant to be read, poems that lose perhaps their essence if we only hear them. This theme of the oral versus the written nature of poetry is something that we will return to often as we trace a history of poetry."

Provide positive feedback about what went well in class.

EXAMPLE "This is an incredibly complex problem set, and at the beginning of class, I said that this would be a difficult review for us to pull off successfully. I am impressed with the way you all stepped up to the challenge."

Although it sounds like an easy thing to do, bringing a class to a meaningful conclusion is an acquired skill. When you first start teaching, your efforts to bring the class to closure may feel awkward; as you gain experience, you will be able to integrate your conclusion more and more naturally into the flow of the class.

▓ Further Reading

Brookfield, S. D. 2006. *The Skillful Teacher: On Technique, Trust, and Responsiveness in the Classroom.* 2d ed. San Francisco: Jossey-Bass.

Davis, B. G. 2009. *Tools for Teaching.* 2d. ed. San Francisco: Jossey-Bass.

Filene, P. 2005. *The Joy of Teaching: A Practical Guide for New College Instructors.* Chapel Hill: University of North Carolina Press.

Lowman, J. 1995. *Mastering the Techniques of Teaching.* 2d ed. San Francisco: Jossey-Bass.

Richner, S., and L. Weir, eds. 1995. *Beyond Political Correctness: Toward the Inclusive University.* Toronto: University of Toronto Press.

Rotenberg, R. 2010. *The Art and Craft of College Teaching: A Guide for New Professors and Graduate Students.* 2d ed. Walnut Creek, CA: Left Coast Press.

Svinicki, M., and W. J. McKeachie. 2011. *McKeachie's Teaching Tips: Strategies, Research, and Theory for College and University Teachers.* 13th ed. Belmont, CA: Wadsworth.

5

Trusty Class Plans

Some course material and class goals lend themselves to more highly structured class plans—more structured than the typical full-class discussion. This chapter provides nine tried-and-true lesson plans, which cover a range of different goals and activities.

▦ Information Exchange

For information exchange students read an assigned segment of course material at home and then present a summary of the readings in class to their classmates.

When to Use It

Information exchanges work very well when you are trying to cover a lot of information quickly and you think that students may not be doing all the reading (or at least not doing all of it very carefully). You are, in a sense, organizing a class study session, and it is often better to have the students learn the information this way than (1) have you lecture to them about it or (2) not learn it at all.

Students can teach each other, and they often learn a lot from it. You are not shirking your duties if students run the class according to a structure you have planned; you already have done plenty of work to create that situation. Smaller informational exchanges can be organized and completed in one class period, but it is usually more effective to have students prepare ahead of time so that they are ready to teach their classmates when they walk into class.

Advance Preparation for the Teaching Assistant

If students are supposed to read, for example, four articles that week, divide the class (or a subsection of the class) into four groups the week before; see the Debate section in this chapter (page 71) for grouping strategies. Assign each group an article, and tell them that the next week they will have a certain amount of time (say, 15 minutes) to help their classmates get the most out of that article. (Remind them that they must read all the articles; they will get more out of the next class if they do.) It often works well to require each group to have a handout for their classmates: it can summarize relevant information, provide questions for other students to answer, list important terms, and so forth. Tell them that if they get it to you the day before, you will copy it and have it ready for class.

Advance Preparation for Students

When you do this activity for the first time, prepare students for their 15 minutes of teaching. Remind them that talking *at* their peers is not interesting and it will be much livelier if they can get the other students involved. Go so far as to suggest activities, such as pair work you have done as a class before, freewriting, or creating lists. Encourage them to make handouts that you will copy before class. Make yourself available to meet with the groups during office hours to go over their teaching plans. It also helps to remind students that they will be graded on the quality of their presentations.

Steps for an Information Exchange

1. Tell groups in what order they will present. You can organize this thematically or draw numbers out of a hat.

2. Ask the presenting group to move to the front of the room where they command attention. It never hurts to require students to move around, and it makes them seem more like the leaders of the class.

3. Keep very close track of time so that you can get to all the presentations. You may want to make a warning "five minutes left" sign to flash at the presenters.

Wrapping Up

At the end of class, you need to synthesize all this information into a more coherent whole. Take a few minutes and talk to students about how their presentations fit together in a larger scheme and what the most important points are. This is a very appropriate time to lecture; they have not heard your voice for the entire class, and even with good presentations, the students need to understand how the pieces fit together. Be sure to compliment them specifically on a job well done. Even when there are shortcomings in the presentations, you need to point out where students have succeeded. Students need to hear a balance of constructive criticism and encouragement from you.

Debate

When to Use It

Debates encourage students to challenge each other's and their own thinking about controversial issues. While debating may seem like a gimmick, the ability to take information and construct a coherent, compelling argument is at the heart of a liberal arts education. Debates may be especially useful in cases in which you think that your students already have firm positions on an issue or when you want to encourage them to make a thoughtful argument for their position. Debates are also a good way for students to hear both sides of an argument where a full discussion might be stifled by students' efforts to be politically correct. Debates are an excellent option when you want to spend less time preparing for class (e.g., during your own academic crunch periods).

Advance Preparation for the Teaching Assistant

To have a debate, you will need to divide students into two groups, each of which will argue for a particular position on the topic you choose. Before the debate, you will need to decide the topic and how you will divide your students into groups.

EXAMPLES Should marijuana be legalized?

Should animals be used for the testing of possible human immunizations?

Should U.S. citizens not born in the United States be allowed to run for president?

Advance Preparation for Students

You may want to remind your students to bring informational materials to class or to examine specific readings before class on the day you are planning to hold a debate. But, because debating can seem like a corny exercise, you may want to wait until the day you are planning to hold a debate to tell students about this class plan. The longer they know about it, the longer they have to decide that they may not feel like participating.

Grouping Strategies

Here are several different strategies for dividing students into groups.

- Divide students into groups by having them number off. This can have the advantage of separating friends who usually sit next to each other in class into different groups. Separating friends is a good idea if you suspect that they will not stay on task or challenge each other's ideas if assigned to the same group.

- Decide before class which students you would like in each group. This method gives you an opportunity to create groups of students who you think will work well together and to put at least one good talker in each group.

- Ask students to divide themselves into two groups. This method may take more time than you want to spend, as students can be slow to take initiative on this type of task.

- Divide the classroom down the middle. This method is efficient, but it gives you less control over who ends up in each group. The advantage of "natural grouping" is that in these groups, students are already comfortable talking among themselves.

Steps for Debates

1. Start by telling the class that you will begin today's discussion with a debate.

2. Divide the students into two groups. Once they are in groups, ask each group to pick a "secretary" to record the group's ideas. Assign each group a position with regard to the debate topic.

3. Give them ten minutes to work together to come up with all of the arguments that they can on behalf of their position. Remind the secretary to take notes.

4. Give the groups a two-minute warning so they know when they need to start wrapping up.

5. Pick one of the groups to start the debate, and instruct the group that will be going first that it is to make the first point by stating and explaining one of its arguments for or against the issue at hand. For example, the first group might say, "Marijuana should be legalized because it can be used to treat some medical disorders," and then briefly explain this position. Groups should select one or two speakers for each point.

6. Instruct the second group that they are to confer with each other and respond to the first group's point. Once the second group responds, give the first group the opportunity to comment on the response.

7. Once the first point has been exhausted, ask the second group to offer a new point.

Throughout this process, it is your job to keep the debate running smoothly. Be sure the groups take turns in making and rebutting points and that no one group or student dominates the debate. You should decide when a point has been exhausted and when to raise a new one.

You also may encourage the students to take turns speaking for their group. For example, the members of each group may take turns stating each point or rebuttal. Be sure to give the groups time to confer with each other before they make or rebut a point if they need the time to consolidate their argument.

Once the debate is under way, you may go one of two ways with it. You do not need to decide in advance; see how the debate is progressing.

Option 1

8. Continue the process of point making, responding, and rebutting for five to ten minutes. Allow this to go on long enough for each group to become involved in arguing carefully for its position but stop the debate before a majority of the important points have been raised.

9. Stop the debate, instruct the groups to reconvene, and ask each group to prepare to argue the opposite position of the one it just argued.

10. Give the groups five minutes to work out the opposing position and then start the debate in the same manner as before.

11. Allow the debate to continue as long as the groups are making thoughtful points but leave at least ten minutes at the end of class to wrap up.

By forcing the students to take the position opposite of the one they just debated, you expand their thinking and almost certainly force them to challenge some of the ideas they held before class. The downside of this format is that it can cut into a smoothly flowing debate.

Option 2

8. Allow the debate to continue until the groups make most of the significant points related to the issue at hand.

9. Stop the debate before your students seem bored with it or the debate activity begins to drag.

When students do not have to change their position on the issue, they may be able to think through one position thoroughly. In addition, by not stopping the debate midway, you allow it to follow a more natural course. The downside of this format is that your students may leave the classroom without challenging their own thinking about the issue.

Your decision to follow Option 1 or Option 2 may rest on the students' familiarity with the material. Decide if the goal of the class is to generate as many ideas on the topic as possible or to generate a coherent, point-by-point argument on the topic.

Wrapping Up

After you stop the debate, ask students to move back to their regular classroom positions. To help them reflect on the results of the debate, you have a few different options.

- Ask your students if they were surprised by any of the arguments or if they have changed their own views on the topic.

- Review with your students the various points and group the arguments under appropriate headings. As you do this, explain to students how they can apply a similar process when constructing the argument for a paper.

- Have your students pick out fallacious or circular arguments. Find out why they think people would make those weak arguments.

- Focus on the politically incorrect arguments. Who makes these arguments? Are they completely wrong, or do they have elements of truth?

- Find the arguments that oppose each other. Talk about the importance of addressing opposing arguments when making a point.

- Find arguments without any clear opposition, and discuss how you would argue against them.

- Acknowledge that these are complex issues that can have reasoned and thoughtful opposing arguments.

Pros and Cons

When to Use It

This is a particularly good exercise to use when you want to bring out a variety of opinions about a controversial topic but you do not have enough time or energy to stage a debate. Pros and Cons can be used to jump-start what you hope will be a more free-flowing discussion. Like debating, Pros and Cons allows students to voice a variety of opinions (even those that are not politically correct) without worrying about being held personally accountable for their views.

Advance Preparation for the Teaching Assistant

Before doing Pros and Cons in your classroom, you need to think of a controversial issue and list arguments on both sides of the issue to ensure the debate can be a balanced one. As with debates, Pros and Cons can help students see the many complex sides of an issue on which they may already have taken a firm position, thus helping them construct a more thoughtful, persuasive argument.

Advance Preparation for Students

The amount of preparation your students will need depends on the topic you have in mind. If you are covering a topic about which students will benefit from having factual information available to them (e.g., "Should Puerto Rico become a U.S. State?"), you should encourage your students to review certain materials before they come to class. If you are covering a topic with which students are already familiar, you won't need to give them advance warning.

Steps for Pros and Cons

1. Divide the board in half, and write PRO on one side and CON on the other.

2. Tell your students the controversial issue that you have in mind and ask them to come up with all of the arguments that someone might make for or against the issue. You can ask them to do this in pairs first and then share with the full class, or you can work with the full class.

3. Be sure that you ask students to give you all of the available arguments, as opposed to asking them their opinions on the topic. This way, students will be liberated to say things that they might otherwise worry will be held against them personally.

4. Write the arguments on the board as they are given to you by the students. Keep your own list in front of you so that you can add important points that the students leave out. You may have to make the first politically incorrect comment in order to get that side of the issue "on the board." If you find your class tiptoeing around politically charged issues, be the first to say, for example, "Well, some people feel that Puerto Rico should not be made a state because most of its citizens are minorities."

5. Continue until you feel both sides of the issue have been exhausted.

Wrapping Up

Once you have extensive lists for both sides of the issue, point out to your students that this is the process through which meaningful arguments (e.g., papers) are composed. They can use a similar process to generate ideas, choose a position, and organize an argument while considering plausible counterarguments. (See page 74 for a list of suggested closing activities.) The advantage with this class plan is that you have all the ideas on the board so that you can physically connect or group them with your chalk or pen.

■ Consolidating Lists

When to Use It

When you have a question with discrete, "listable" answers, this class plan can be an effective way to generate discussion. It works particularly well with a topic that seems at first glance too abstract to define but that can, in fact, be characterized (e.g., good writing). This exercise also helps students sift through and prioritize ideas and arguments. It is inherently artificial to ask students to come up with a certain number of answers; it is perfectly appropriate for you to recognize that fact when you introduce the activity, but it is not a reason to dismiss the exercise.

EXAMPLES List ten characteristics of good writing.

List five possible arguments against the English Language Amendment.

List six potential flaws in a sociological study like the one in the article.

Advance Preparation for the Teaching Assistant

All you need to do ahead of time is think of the question, decide how many points to put on the list, and decide how many times you want to consolidate lists. You should also make your own list in your class plan so that you can be sure that students cover all of the points you think are important.

Steps for Consolidating Lists

1. Ask each student to get out a piece of paper and explain the list you would like them to create.

2. Give students five to ten minutes to complete their lists.

3. When all of the students have lists, put them in pairs and tell them to consolidate their two lists into one with the original number of items. They must, therefore, decide which items can be combined and which items are more important than others.

4. Optional: Next, put the pairs into groups of four and ask them to consolidate the two lists into one. At this point, they will begin to identify common threads. You also can ask them to rank these elements in order of importance.

Wrapping Up

The easiest way to bring this exercise back to a full-class discussion is to create a class list on the board. With you as the transcriber, ask each group to provide one or two items for the master list. Once you reach the designated number, ask for additional items; as a class, determine whether they should displace or be combined with an item already on the board. When the list is finished, you can talk to the class about how this exercise proves how much shared knowledge we do or do not possess about what is important or characteristic of this given issue.

You also can use any of the suggested activities in Wrapping Up in the Debate section of this chapter (page 74).

▥ Video Presentation

Before you plan the viewing of a video into your syllabus, check with the media center at your institution to learn the policy for showing films in the classroom for educational purposes.

When to Use It

Showing a video or a movie can bring a perspective into your classroom that is not available in other ways. Your goal can be purely to provide information (a documentary about South African politics), to supply a needed example (a feature film with an excellent example of psychopathology), or to introduce a novel viewpoint (labor relations from the perspective of the union workers' families).

Advance Preparation for the Teaching Assistant

Watch the movie or program at least once before showing it to the class. Be sure it will fit into the time allotted. If not, determine what parts you can skip. Decide which points or themes you think the students should focus on as they watch. Prepare questions for your students that fit the goal you had in mind when you chose the video material; you can either put these questions on a handout that you distribute at the beginning of class or keep them for a full-class discussion after the video.

Reserve the necessary equipment: TV, DVD/VCR, and so forth. Get to class early that day to make sure everything is there and working.

Advance Preparation for Students

Unfortunately, some students think of a day with video material as a nonrequired class. Tell your students that you will be showing a video at least a week before you plan to do so, and explain why it is important for them to see it (this way, they will not see the projector or TV and turn tail). Your job is to show and enforce for students how these programs or films are educational because students' immediate reaction will be to leave or, if they stay, to sit back, relax, turn off their brains, and enjoy the show. The week before, mention some incentive for watching the video carefully (an assignment, the final exam, etc.).

Steps for a Video Presentation

1. You will want to introduce the video material either in the previous class or just prior to showing the movie or both. Remember, it is your responsibility to frame this as an educational experience. Tell them about the director, the making of the production, its relevance to the course, and so on.

2. If possible, help students to watch and talk about the video critically. Ask students to take notes during the movie or write about their reflections afterward in response to questions from your handout. You also can ask students to write responses to the movie for homework (either general responses or responses to a specific question that you pose).

Wrapping Up

A post-video discussion can cover questions from the handout or questions that you prepared in advance. This is also a good time to talk about how useful students found the video, if they felt that it challenged or expanded their thinking, and how you envisioned the video enhancing other course material.

Guest Speaker

When to Use Them

Guest speakers are especially helpful when you are dealing with a topic that would be enhanced by the perspective of someone who has very specific experience in the area. Depending on your field, a guest speaker might be a fellow graduate student who does research in the area of interest, the director of the local recycling plant, a dissident from a country discussed in your course, or an ex-convict. Be creative when thinking about the kind of speakers that could enhance the teaching in your course!

Advance Preparation for the Teaching Assistant

You will only want to invite guest speakers who will be able to speak thoughtfully and effectively in front of your students. Although you may know a fascinating person who is also an accomplished environmentalist, you will not want to invite them to speak to your class on natural resources if they are painfully shy in front of groups. Often, you will be able to find guest speakers who are accustomed to speaking to large groups, but if you have any concerns about the person you would like to invite, do not hesitate to ask them how they feel about speaking in front of 30 students for an hour.

Once you have selected a guest speaker, talk with them about what kind of presentation will work for your class. Be sure to cover these points:

- how long the guest speaker will speak (e.g., the entire class period, only 15 minutes)
- how their talk fits in with the structure of the course
- whether they should be prepared to answer questions from your students
- what your students already know about the topic
- particular interests your students have expressed.

Advance Preparation for Students

Let your students know in advance when you will have a guest speaker. If you plan to have the speaker take questions from students, ask students to write questions as a homework assignment before the speaker arrives. This forces the students to prepare for the presentation, allows you to ensure that there are questions, and can help your speaker to prepare their presentation. Also, remind your students that the speaker is a guest of the class, so, *of course*, they will arrive at class on time and give the speaker their full attention for the duration of the period.

Steps for a Class with a Guest Speaker

1. Begin class by dealing with minor class business (if necessary) and then introduce the speaker. Tell students the format for the presentation (e.g., whether there will be time left at the end of class for questions).

2. Turn the class over to the guest speaker. Your advance preparation with the guest speaker should make for a thoughtful, appropriate, and interesting presentation. If it turns out that your guest speaker is pitching their talk too high, too low, or in the wrong place altogether for your students, you must wait patiently until a natural break occurs in the presentation for an opportunity to help the speaker focus on the useful subjects for your class.

3. If questions from the class or a whole-class discussion are included as part of the presentation, it is your job to call on students or to moderate the discussion unless the

speaker indicates otherwise. It is always a good idea to have a few questions of your own prepared in case the discussion needs a jump start.

4. It is your job to end class on time. When the end of class arrives, thank your speaker for coming and tell your students to hold any unanswered questions; you can find time in the following week to discuss them as a class.

Wrapping Up

It is always a good idea to send your guest speaker a note thanking them for their contributions to your class. If time and logistics allow, bring a card with you to the next class and ask students to sign the thank you note before you send it.

In the first class meeting after you have had a guest speaker, ask your students what they thought about the presentation and what they found useful, surprising, or unsettling. While you may want to put a time limit on this discussion so that you can get on to the rest of your class plan, it is important to get feedback from your students about the speaker before you decide whether to invite the same speaker back next semester.

Lecture

When to Use It

Lectures are useful when you want to introduce students to new material as efficiently as possible. In an information intensive course, you may find yourself with a list of points that need to be explained to supplement the general lecture; another lecture or a mini-lecture for part of the class may be the most effective way to impart the information.

Advance Preparation for the Teaching Assistant

Lecturing requires a great deal of advance preparation on the part of the instructor; the steps for preparing for a lecture class are detailed in the next section (pages 83–85). Despite the advance legwork, you should not assume that "lecturing" means that you will simply talk at your students for the duration of the class period. Often, the best lectures are those that invite student participation and questions. If possible, take advantage of the smaller size of a class to encourage students to be active in the learning process, even on lecture days. However, if the course material on a given day requires you to lecture without much student participation, be sure to alert your students that you are departing from your usual format and briefly explain your reasons for doing so.

Steps for Preparing a Lecture

1. Select the learning objectives for your lecture. Learning objectives focus on the new content or the new skills students should master by the end of the course. Learning objectives address the question: "What do students need to know about this subject?" not "What do I know about this subject?"

   EXAMPLES To recognize, describe, and order Kohlberg's stages of moral development.

   To identify the systematic features of the Jamaican dialect.

   To understand how multiple systems function simultaneously to create pipelining in computer science.

2. Develop your lecture. To give an effective lecture, you will need to plan everything you intend to say. Some instructors prefer to write out the entire lecture; others create a detailed outline. Either way, do not approach writing your lecture the same way you would approach writing an academic article. Compared to a piece of academic writing, your lecture should be more conversational and less dense. When information is delivered aurally, we all benefit from repetition, anecdotes, narrative explanations, lots of signposting (signals about where you are and where you are going), and as much interaction as possible.

3. Find a hook for your lecture topic. In other words, think of a way to engage students in your lecture topic as soon as class begins and at various points along the way. Bear in mind that you have been thinking about your lecture for several days while your students arrive in class with little sense of what to expect for the day. Also remember that listening to a lecture is hard work and that it's not stooping to include various gimmicks as a way to keep your students engaged.

EXAMPLES   Write several questions on the board that the students will be able to answer by the end of the lecture.

Stream images, music, or video relevant to the lecture topic as students arrive for class.

Begin class or a given section of the lecture by asking students to share examples or experiences relevant to the lecture topic.

4. After you have written your lecture notes, practice the lecture, several times. You can do this in front of a mirror or quietly at your desk. Practicing your lecture helps ensure that the lecture fits with the time parameters you have available and also prevents you from reading the lecture to your students when you get to class. Having practiced your lecture several times, you should be able to deliver the lecture simply by glancing at your notes.

5. Develop a broad outline of your lecture to share with your students. Having a broad outline handy will help your students to follow your lecture more effectively and gain a better sense of how the material you are presenting hangs together. At the beginning of the outline you provide to your students, list your learning objectives.

Sharing the Lecture Outline with Students

Once you have created the broad outline for the lecture, you can distribute it to students in at least two ways.

- Type the outline, copy it, and hand it out to students at the beginning of class.

  PROS   Students will have your entire outline at the beginning of class.

  Students may choose to use your handout as a place to take notes.

  A handout can save you from having to write the outline on the board or worry about any of the technology snags that can occur with overheads or PowerPoint presentations.

  CONS   Students may choose to rewrite the handout content into their own notes, meaning that they may miss some of the lecture as they copy the handout material.

  Handouts lack any of the high-tech frills that come with PowerPoint (color images, streaming video, etc.). They also kill trees.

- Post the outline on Blackboard or some other course management system and ask students to bring it to class.

  PROS   Students come to class oriented to the plan for the day.

  Students can tailor the formatting of the outline to their own note-taking style.

  CONS   The lecture and its outline will need to be prepared well in advance to give students the opportunity to download the outline. (This might also be a Pro.)

  Some students will likely forget to download the outline so you will need to have extra copies on hand.

  Students may feel that they already have, or can easily acquire, all the information they need for the day and become disengaged.

Delivering Your Lecture

It's easy to generate a mental image of a tedious lecture, and certainly we've all sat through many lectures where we spent a lot of time looking at the clock. While students may have come to expect lectures to be fairly boring and/or full of overwhelming detail, this need not be the case.

- Use body language to connect with your audience. Look at your students, keep your hands out of your pockets, and move around (but not frantically so).

- Take advantage of lecturing as the medium in which it is appropriate to "tell a story" about something in your field. Students learn through narratives.

- Treat your lecture as a conversation with your class. Make it clear that you expect students to ask questions as they arise and encourage audience participation. Feel free to interrupt yourself and talk directly to a particular student if you see a student looking puzzled or having an "aha!" moment.

- Use activities, props, stories, anecdotes, metaphors, examples, images, and/or videos throughout your lecture to keep students engaged and keep the pace of the lecture lively.

    EXAMPLES To teach the concept of pipelining in computer science, send pieces of paper down a row of students with each student drawing their own shape and passing on the paper each time you snap your fingers. They will then see the simultaneous functioning of many parts of a multiple task.

    "This mathematical relationship can be paralleled to the codependence of foxes and bunnies. A certain number of foxes eat a certain number of bunnies to survive. Now, what happens to the bunnies if the fox population suddenly grows larger?"

- Personalize examples, involve your audience.

  EXAMPLE   "Say that Hannah here in the front row is a
             farmer who needs to use the fences she has
             available to enclose the largest space possible.
             Hannah is not expecting to use calculus to
             solve this problem, but we're going to use cal-
             culus. How do we go about converting the
             information about fields and fences into cal-
             culus symbols?"

Using Technology

Many instructors rely on PowerPoint to deliver course content during lectures. We know PowerPoint is "sexy" and often convenient,
but we encourage you to consider the following pros and cons of
using it.

  PROS   PowerPoint provides a convenient way to store and
         present video clips, digital images, graphs, and charts.

         PowerPoint presentations can save the instructor from
         having to write the lecture content on the board or
         provide it on an overhead or handout.

         PowerPoint presentations can be edited right up to
         the moment class starts.

  CONS   PowerPoint moves too fast for students (or any
         human mind!). Either students are too busy copying
         slide content to process your lecture, or students,
         expecting the slides to be available after class, men-
         tally check out.

         PowerPoint restricts the instructor's ability to be spon-
         taneous in the presentation of the material or to
         shape the lecture in response to students' questions
         and needs.

         PowerPoint can fail if a technology problem occurs.

         PowerPoint can tempt the instructor to read from
         their slides (and it just doesn't get much more boring
         than that).

Wrapping Up

At the end of your lecture, return to the learning objectives that you articulated at the beginning of class. Point out to your students how the learning objectives have been achieved, invite questions pertaining to the learning objectives if time allows, and—if appropriate—alert students to how the content you covered in the lecture connects to other areas of the course content.

▣ Exam Preparation

When to Use It

If you plan to devote all or most of a class to preparing your students for an exam, do so in the last class meeting before an exam is administered. Although it would be wonderful to help students prepare for an exam two weeks in advance, it is not practical. It is a rare college student who begins to study for an exam more than a few days before they have to take it.

Some teaching assistants feel that they are pandering to grade-grubbing students when they devote class time to exam preparation, but taking time for this kind of review is exactly the purpose of giving exams in the first place. Exams provide an excellent opportunity to encourage students to consolidate and synthesize what they have learned in your course by capitalizing on their motivation to do well on the exam. In addition, exam taking is an academic skill like any other. When you teach students exam preparation skills, you help them recognize and remember what is important in your course.

Advance Preparation for the Teaching Assistant

You will need to go over all the material that will be covered on the exam to make sure that it all makes sense to you. If you choose Option 1 from the following set of options, make copies of an old exam to hand out to your students in the class meeting before the exam preparation session. If you choose Option 2, leave time to create a handout of student questions.

Advance Preparation for Students

How you ask students to prepare for the exam preparation session will dictate how you run the session itself. Choose one or two options that will work best for the material you will review.

Option 1

If you have copies of old exams that are similar to the one you will administer, ask your students to work through the old exams before the exam preparation session and take note of areas where they have difficulty. If you are uncomfortable giving out an old exam, check to see if students have access to one anyway. Many fraternities, sororities, and other student groups save old exams. In this case, not distributing an old exam may only penalize students who do not have access to it. If you are working with a professor who writes the exams for the course, don't distribute old exams without first checking with the professor.

Option 2

Before the exam preparation session, ask students to review the material the exam will cover and write three questions they would ask if they were writing the exam. They must get these questions to you (in your box or by email) two days before the preparation session.

Option 3

Before the exam preparation session, ask students to review the material and come up with specific questions about areas that they do not understand. Tell your students that you will be happy to clarify any topic for them but that you will not answer questions like, "What parts of the text do you think we should study?"

With any of these three options, you can spend part of the class period talking with students about test-taking strategies. For example, you can talk over with students how to write a successful in-class essay (e.g., foregrounding your main point), what counts as "explaining the significance" of a literary passage in a passage identification section, and so on. Many of them will probably be willing to share their successful (or dramatically unsuccessful!) strategies both for studying and for taking similar exams.

Steps for Exam Preparation

The steps that you use for your exam preparation session will depend on the options you chose from those listed previously.

Option 1

1. Give your students the correct answers to the sample exam on a handout. Or, ask pairs of students to compare their answers and look for discrepancies.

2. Ask students to ask specific questions about areas where they struggled on the sample exam.

3. Encourage students to help each other toward the correct answers and clarify any controversies about the material. If no one in the class seems to know a given answer, give the answer to the class. Even if similar material will be covered on the upcoming exam, what counts is that the students learn and remember it!

4. Work through as many questions as you can in the time available.

Option 2

1. Prepare a handout with as many of the students' questions as you feel are appropriate (you may need to consolidate some questions or add a few of your own).

2. Put students in groups of three or four to work through the questions together. Be available to answer groups' questions as they go.

3. Bring the discussion back to the full class to review questions that caused trouble.

4. Finally, ask students to volunteer additional questions that did not come up and go over them as a class.

Option 3

1. Begin class by reminding your students that you will limit the preparation session to answering specific questions; your students should not expect you to summarize the exam material for them.

2. Field questions from your students one at a time. Solicit input from the class on each question, but answer questions where no one has the correct answer or too much time will be spent on getting the correct answer.

3. Continue to take questions on the exam material for as long as the class period allows, or until they run out of specific questions.

Wrapping Up

Regardless of the option you choose, you will want to keep track of the topics that are addressed in the exam preparation session and note any areas of the material that will be on the exam that were not adequately addressed in the preparation session. Remind students about these important topics and encourage them to study those areas also.

Grammar and Usage Review

When to Use It

In a course in which you are reading student writing, you may find yourself becoming frustrated by recurring usage problems. This activity is a quick and easy way to review and correct common usage mistakes.

When you do this exercise, you can remind students that part of "good" grammar is mastering a set of written conventions. The written language differs from the spoken, and your students may not always be able to find a logic to a particular written convention; but in many contexts, they will be judged by their control of these grammatical usage rules. Setting up written grammar in this way can make this exercise seem more like a challenging game than a test of the students' intellect or fluency.

Advance Preparation for the Teaching Assistant

Select eight to ten sentences from your students' writing that exemplify the problems you want to tackle. You may need to alter students' sentences slightly or make up a couple of examples. Using actual student writing makes the exercise seem less abstract, and students usually find the usage issues in their own writing to be more amusing than embarrassing (and the sentences are anonymous unless a student opts to claim ownership during class).

Keep the sentences fairly short so that the students do not become distracted from the targeted usage questions. Choose your sentences thematically: do not try to cover ten different usage problems; select two or three problems instead (e.g., comma splices, lack of parallelism, dangling modifiers) and use the sentences to cover different variations of these problems.

Create a handout using these sentences (without the student authors' names). Make sure to leave space between the sentences so that students can add their corrections.

Sentence Revision (a.k.a. Usage Questions)

Revise the following sentences so that they are clear and no longer contain usage problems. (Some of these sentences should look familiar!)

1. The comparison of two simultaneous trials should identify any idiosyncratic problems with the sample collection, this methodology helps to ensure more accurate results.

2. The artist captures the serenity of the scene in the diffusion of soft colors; although the overlaid short brush strokes imbue the painting with living vitality.

3. The governor has tried to defend his actions, however, his press secretary has tried to pretend the incident never occurred.

Steps for Grammar and Usage Review

1. Explain to the students why you have decided they will benefit from a review of usage questions and give them an explicit time limit for the exercise if you are planning to cover other material that day.

2. Give each student a copy of the handout and ask them to work in pairs to revise the sentences. This strategy allows students to compare grammatical knowledge and answer some of their own questions.

3. While students are working, put numbers on the board or overhead for the number of sentences on the handout, leaving space for students to write the corrected sentences.

4. After five minutes, walk around the room and ask various pairs to put a revised version of the sentence on the board when they are ready.

5. As a class, discuss the revised versions of the sentences. Ask students for other possible revisions or for other questions that come to mind.

6. If time allows, ask students what other grammatical issues have been giving them trouble.

Wrapping Up

Tell students that you expect never to see any of these problems again in their writing. They laugh, you laugh, and you hope that at least they understand a little more about usage conventions than they did before they walked into the classroom. Then move on to the next class activity.

Essay Workshop

When to Use It

If students are writing an essay for your class and you want to emphasize the process of writing (drafts and revision), workshops are an effective way to make students put more time into their writing. Students work in small groups (three or four students) to help each other improve their drafts. Because they will have read the essays beforehand and made written comments, the workshop involves talking about the drafts rather than reading them.

Advance Preparation for the Teaching Assistant

Create workshop groups; you can announce these when you give the essay assignment. Groups of three work best, but groups of four are also possible. The directions that follow assume your students will be working in groups of three. If you know the students' writing, try to put at least one strong writer in each group to act both as a model for the other students and as a trusty peer responder.

Before the first workshop, you should provide guidelines about how students should compose their written responses to drafts of other students' essays and about how the workshop is supposed to run.

Create a schedule of due dates: draft due date (when students will give their drafts to the other members of their group); workshop date (a few days after the draft due date when students will come prepared with their written responses to the two other papers in their group); final essay due date.

Emphasize to students their responsibility for the success of this activity. They must have their drafts ready, and they must be present in class for the workshop. You may want to stress repercussions for missing the workshop, as this will inevitably doom the group's effectiveness and is not fair to the student's peers.

If the draft due date is a class day, have students exchange papers at the beginning or end of class. If the draft due date has to be a nonclass day, make sure that students have each other's email addresses and phone numbers so that they can contact each other and make the exchange.

Before the first workshop, discuss how the workshop should unfold. You may want to hold a practice full-class workshop with an essay from another class you have taught or from another teaching assistant so that students can see how a workshop should progress; you can ask one student to pretend to be the author (or volunteer yourself) so that the other students direct their (sensitive and constructive) comments to an "author figure." Encourage them to provide positive comments along with constructive suggestions. You can also provide written workshop guidelines for students.

> See Appendix E for a sample set of written guidelines and further information about how to run a essay workshop.

Advance Preparation for Students

Students must have the drafts of their essays prepared by the draft due date and should bring three copies of their draft to class that day: one for themselves and one for each of the other people in their workshop group. You may opt to have them make a copy for you also, but be very clear about whether you are planning to read it or whether you are simply checking to make sure they have written it.

Students will take the other two students' papers home and write a peer response to each, commenting on the argument, tone, organization, and so forth. When students come to class on the day of the workshop, they will bring two copies of each response: one for the student writer and one for you (you probably will want to grade these responses so that students put time and effort into them).

Provide students with a set of guidelines about how to write these responses to other students' essays. Emphasize that they should focus first on the big issues (the argument, organization) and only later on punctuation and grammar (if it even becomes relevant). Explain how long the response should be (one to two pages works well) and how you will grade it.

> See Appendix F for a sample set of guidelines for writing a peer response.

Steps for Essay Workshops

1. On the day of the workshop, ask students to pull out their copy of their own essays. Give them a few minutes to write at the top of their papers three questions they would like to ask their peer responders (e.g., "How can I fix the conclusion?").

2. Put the students into their groups, remind them of their task, and let them go at it. Tell them about how long they should spend on each paper. Encourage them to look at their drafts of and responses to the one student's paper but not to read their written responses verbatim to the student; the student can read the responses at home later—the workshop is a time for two-way dialogue.

3. Walk around the room and keep an eye on the progress of all the groups. Feel free to join in a group for a few minutes if the participants seem to be struggling or having a disagreement.

Wrapping Up

When all the groups have finished discussing the papers, remind students of the due date for the final draft. If you are willing to meet with students about their papers before then, you may want to stipulate that they must revise the draft after the workshop before they talk to you about it.

Grading

Grade the written responses to ensure that students put some time and care into them. You may want to use grades or a simple number system (e.g., 1–5). If you choose to collect the first drafts, you will have to decide whether you want to grade these for effort or simply to refer to them when grading the final versions. Obviously, students benefit from getting your written feedback on paper drafts, but there are serious drawbacks to doing so.

- Reading and commenting on two drafts of a paper takes an inordinate amount of your time.
- Students may dismiss their peers' comments on the draft, waiting only for your comments.
- Students often believe that if they respond to all of your written comments on the draft (and no more), they will get an A. As this is often not the case, they may feel misled.

An effective alternative for helping students with paper drafts is arranging individual meetings with students during your office hours to discuss their papers. You can offer to skim through drafts and provide general feedback that will help students rewrite their work.

An Optional Final Class Exercise for an Essay Workshop

Most students make no distinction between revising and editing. The workshop will help them to see that revision can involve a structural overhaul, the addition or subtraction of ideas, the reworking of the introduction, and so forth. If you want to teach them a lesson about editing—about the importance of proofreading for good presentation—try this exercise.

Steps for This Final Exercise

1. On the day the essay is due, pair up students and ask them to exchange papers. (They will groan, but you can explain that if anyone has a perfect paper at the end of the class, you will be happy to take it. If not, they have a chance to fix it.)

2. Ask them to proofread each other's papers for grammar and punctuation. Ask every student to give their partner permission to write on their paper. Encourage them to go slowly, to read aloud if they want to.

3. Provide them with a proofreading guide sheet of common problems if you have one prepared.

4. Make yourself available for any and all usage questions that may arise.

5. Determine whether anyone has an unmarked paper. If so, collect it. If not, tell the students that they have until the next day to fix the problems and get the paper into your mailbox.

This exercise works wonderfully the first time because students are not expecting it and they come to class with final drafts. Once the element of surprise is gone, however, they tend to use this editing session as a second revision session, and they do not come prepared with final drafts.

Proofreading Guide Sheet

Here is a list of some common problems to watch for when you *edit* your draft, *after you have revised it:*

1. ***This/That***   When these words stand alone at the beginning of a sentence, their reference is sometimes unclear; putting a noun after *this* or *that* (e.g., *this fact* or *this situation*) can help make the reference clear.

2. **Verb tense**   Pay attention to verb tense. Do not change tense randomly.

3. **Comma splices** Commas cannot connect two independent clauses alone (semicolons can).

4. ***You***   If you use *you* in the paper, make sure that you have a reason for directly addressing the audience at that particular point in the paper.

(And so on)

Further Reading

Cannon, R., and D. Newble. 2000. *A Handbook for Teachers in Universities and Colleges: A Guide to Improving Teaching Methods.* 4th ed. London: Kogan Page.

Davis, B. G. 2009. *Tools for Teaching.* 2d. ed. San Francisco: Jossey-Bass.

Halpern, D. F., and associates. 1994. *Changing College Classrooms: New Teaching and Learning Strategies for an Increasingly Complex World.* San Francisco: Jossey-Bass.

Hedengren, B. F. 2004. *A TA's Guide to Teaching Writing in All Disciplines.* Boston: Bedford/St. Mark's.

Meyers, C. 1993. *Promoting Active Learning: Strategies for the College Classroom.* San Francisco: Jossey-Bass.

Rotenberg, R. 2010. *The Art and Craft of College Teaching: A Guide for New Professors and Graduate Students.* 2d ed. Walnut Creek, CA: Left Coast Press.

Svinicki, M., and W. J. McKeachie. 2011. *McKeachie's Teaching Tips: Strategies, Research, and Theory for College and University Teachers.* 13th ed. Belmont, CA: Wadsworth.

Tufte, E.R. 2006. *The Cognitive Style of Powerpoint: Pitching Out Corrupts Within.* 2d ed. Chesire: Graphics Press.

"What questions do you have . . . . . . ?

04/03/2016.

6

Designing Student Assignments

The key to helping students produce good work is designing good assignments. As they say, "Garbage in, garbage out." This chapter covers teaching with problem sets, conducting experimental laboratories, developing essay assignments, and creating exams.

▣ Teaching with Problem Sets

Most mathematics courses and many courses in the natural sciences require students to complete problem sets on a regular basis. All courses in foreign languages require students to complete practice exercises. In the remainder of this section, the term *problem set* is used to apply to any assignment of questions students are expected to answer.

Problem sets are important and useful as a tool through which students acquire skills and demonstrate an understanding of larger concepts. Your teaching of problem sets should reinforce this relationship between problem sets (the "hands-on part") and the material of the course (the "abstract part"). Your job is not over when students have all the correct answers to a problem set in hand; they must also understand the concept behind the answers and how this concept could be applied to other problems.

For courses with problem sets, much of the section or the course itself will involve reviewing or otherwise incorporating these homework assignments. The key is to find ways to make this activity productive and participatory—an active learning experience for the students.

Framing the Purpose of Problem Sets

Many students walk into math, science, and language classes expecting the focus to be on right and wrong answers. Instructors reinforce this expectation when their sole focus in these classes seems to be on correct answers. Although accuracy is, of course, critical to math, science, and language learning, you need to stress for yourself and for your students the importance of good problem solving over perfect solutions. In the educational process, the key is often the journey, not the destination; students need to be able to chart their way through new problems in the future without your assistance.

From the beginning of the semester, make it clear to your students that you are an instructor who believes in the importance of persistence and risk taking as much as correct answers. For students to take this statement seriously, you need to structure the course so that it emphasizes the problem-solving process.

In lower-level courses, students will often come in with vastly different backgrounds, particularly in math. You will undoubtedly encounter "math anxiety" in at least a few students; you may find this kind of anxiety to be more common with female students entering the sciences, which have historically been male-dominated disciplines (but this is changing). You may overhear students explaining their dislike or lack of success with comments such as, "I'm just bad at math." It is important for you to remember that the same problem set can be simple for some students and almost impossible for others, and that competent students may feel doubtful of their abilities.

At the beginning of the semester, gauge the range of abilities and experience in the class. Emphasize to all students that *everyone* has to put in time and hard work to succeed in these fields. Make yourself available to provide support for those students who need it (and who are willing to work for it). However, you cannot emphasize enough that it is up to the students to learn the material; you cannot do it for them.

Framing the Assessment of Problem Sets

In math and in the sciences, exams are often graded on a curve, which can accurately and fairly reflect students' relative mastery of difficult material. With problem sets, you may want to dispense with a grading curve in order to encourage collaborative learning and create a more supportive learning community among the students. Find out your department's policy about encouraging and grading group work. Assuming group work is acceptable, encourage students to seek outside help (tutors, classmates, you); in the end, however, the work must be their own. Tell them you expect they will be able to explain the solution to *any* problem they answer. Remind them that they will be working individually on exams.

You may not have the power to determine how students are graded in section or to create extra graded assignments. If it is possible for you to develop a grading scheme, use quizzes (five- to ten-minute events) to encourage students to come to class prepared and to assess where students stand with respect to the material.

You can also consider developing a system that credits students for learning activities in which they demonstrate initiative, persistence, risk taking, and overall hard work. For example, you can create a system in which students receive credit for creating study sheets for exams (and turning them in), doing extra homework assignments or "stumper" problems, and giving class presentations. Enough credit at the end of the term can boost a borderline grade.

See pages 136–37 in Chapter 7, Grading Problem Sets, for more information on how to assess student work.

Instructor-Led Review of Problem Sets

There are probably as many different variations on ways to review problem sets as there are different kinds of problem sets. A few general types of reviews with sample lesson plans and guidelines are presented here.

At times, it is most efficient and effective for the teaching assistant to lead the problem set review. Encourage as much student participation in this process as possible.

Steps for the Review

1. Start by establishing the goals for the review: for example, how many problems you expect to cover and how thoroughly, and how students should be involved in the review process.

2. Begin with a problem of your choosing or ask students to decide which problem they would like to cover first.

3. If a student chooses the problem, ask them where they got stuck and then determine how many other students got stuck at this same point. If you have chosen the problem, poll the class on where they ran into difficulties.

4. Once you have determined the area(s) of difficulty, respond with questions to the class (not just to the student asking the question) about how to begin working on a solution. You may want to ask them to choose among several options about how to proceed; if you offer only one suggestion, most students will agree to it, whether it is the most helpful option or not.

   EXAMPLES   "Do you want to draw a picture?"

   "Do you want to work backward from the answer?"

   "Do you want to solve a simpler problem first?"

   "Do you want to substitute easier numbers for harder ones in the equation?"

5. If one student in the class has figured out how to do the problem and volunteers this information, you can ask them to explain the solution to their classmates if they are comfortable doing so.

   > See pages 105–7 in this chapter, Student Presentations, for more information on spontaneous student teaching.

6. As you continue to review more problems, you may find that you want to be more thorough in your responses to the first few questions and then provide more summary or specific help with later questions.

7. End the review by telling students how you expect them to follow up on this material: for example, correct the problem set and turn it in next class; take five minutes and write down lingering questions so you can know where there is still confusion; try the next few (perhaps harder) problems in the book to see if they can apply their new understanding.

Guidelines for the Review

- Use questions from students to focus your teaching efforts. They are showing you what they do not understand and where they need your assistance.

- Never humiliate students who ask questions, however simple. They (and their classmates) will only be reluctant to ask again if they feel singled out for having revealed their confusion or lack of understanding.

- Be conscious of how much and how often different students are talking and encourage equal participation by students of different genders, races, and ages.

- Because class time is precious, do not feel you have to work through the entire solution. If you know what caused the confusion, you can clarify that aspect of the problem and then allow students to complete their work independently.

- Remember that your goal is not simply to provide correct answers to the assigned problems but rather to foster your students' conceptual understanding.

Student Collaboration in Class

Students learn effectively from each other when working through problem sets. Different students understand different aspects and applications of concepts, and they can often explain them in ways their peers can understand. Do not hesitate to employ group learning during class.

Steps for Group Collaboration

1. Put students into groups of three or four students.

   > See page 71 in Chapter 5, Grouping Strategies, for more information on assigning students to groups.

2. Assign or hand out a set of problems and tell students how many problems they should try to do and how far along toward the answer they should try to get.

3. Walk around the room while students work and encourage them to work together, rather than sitting together and working alone. Feel free to sit down and participate in the solution of a problem, particularly if a group is struggling. Make yourself available to all groups to answer questions.

4. During the session, determine which groups have a solid understanding of which problems.

5. At the end of class, you can ask representatives from various groups to explain their solutions to the class. For example, one student can write out the problem on the board while another provides a "play-by-play" explanation.

Steps for Pair Collaboration

1. Put students into pairs.

2. Assign or hand out a set of problems and tell students how many problems they should try to do and how far along toward the answer they should try to get.

3. Have one student be the "talker" and the other be the "listener." The talker must explain to the listener (who can always ask questions) how they would work through a problem or set of problems.

4. Halfway through the session, students should switch roles.

5. Leave time at the end of class for a full-class review of at least a few problems. Choose one or more problems and ask the listeners to volunteer their partner if their partner provided a clear and detailed answer; if so, ask the talker to speak to the entire class (they have the advantage and confidence of having practiced the explanation once).

Guidelines for In-Class Collaboration

- Inevitably, some groups will contain students with similar levels of understanding, while other groups will have a wide range of abilities. It is important, therefore, that you keep reshuffling groups during the term so that students do not get trapped in particular roles within a group's dynamic (e.g., talker, listener).

- Find out your department's policy on encouraging and grading group work if the in-class work will be graded.

- Be very clear and explicit about what you expect and allow in terms of collaboration, both inside and outside of class. Students may come to your class with different expectations for how much collaboration is permissible on graded work.

- Be vigilant about keeping all group members engaged in the problem solving. Since they will be working individually on exams, they need to develop their own skills as well as their ability to work in groups.

- Some students work better alone and prefer to do their work that way. Different students benefit from different learning methods; you will be helpful to the greatest number of students if you vary your class plans from week to week.

Student Presentations

Student presentations reinforce the importance of risk taking and help create a learning community in which the process is valued as much as the product. Students can present completed problems to the class either on a spontaneous basis or with advance preparation.

Steps for Student Presentations

1. At the beginning of the term, establish a set number of points students will receive for a presentation (or credit that will go toward their participation grade). Tell students they always get full credit for a presentation as long as they have the material prepared; reinforce that they do not have to be correct but they do have to be prepared to talk through the solution. They must be able both to re-create

the solution on the board (or overhead projector) and to explain it as they go.

2. Tell students at the beginning of the term that they should be prepared to be corrected if necessary during their presentation in exchange for full presentation credit, given appropriate preparation. Again, you can remind students that they are working with difficult material and that if they already had it perfectly mastered, they wouldn't be in the class. Emphasize the process and risk taking.

3. For a spontaneous student presentation, ask the class if anyone is prepared to present a solution to a problem that another student has asked about. If so, turn over the front of the room to the student who feels prepared to present the solution. After you do this a few times, students will begin to prepare problems for presentation while they are doing their homework.

4. To organize students for prepared presentations of a problem set during the next session, ask which specific problems students do not understand or select a few problems you think will be particularly difficult for them. Then ask if there are any volunteers to present solutions for those problems in the next class. Make yourself available to those students for help before the next class so that they can feel confident making the presentation.

5. Once you turn over the front of the classroom to the student presenter, seat yourself near the front (perhaps off to one side) where you are available to help but not a dominant presence.

6. Be prepared to step in to correct mistakes if the presenter's classmates do not see the mistakes or are unwilling to correct them.

7. After a student presentation, thank the presenter for their work and, if applicable, point out strengths in their solution and presentation so that other students can identify key components of the process.

Guidelines for Student Presentations

- Alleviate as much anxiety as you can for student presenters by continually reinforcing that you see presentations as a useful way to assess student understanding.
- Stress that students always get full credit for the presentation as long as they have material prepared, even if the presentation is not perfect.
- Set yourself up as a support system for presentations, not a judge; students should know they can look to you for guidance if they are feeling lost or anxious during the presentation, particularly early in the term.

Running an Experimental Lab

Many courses in departments such as physics, biology, chemistry, or natural resources incorporate experimental labs into the teaching of the material. Teaching any particular lab requires a great deal of highly specific information and expertise in the relevant area. This section will address only general information applicable to experimental labs in most natural sciences.

Weekly Preparation

Many teaching assistants meet in weekly preparation sections with the course professor or laboratory instructor. In these sessions, the professor typically discusses the upcoming experiment, notes potential problems, and answers questions. The professor often addresses issues related to lab equipment, supplies, and safety. Use these sessions to familiarize yourself with the laboratory procedure and with the professor's expectations.

If it is possible, you should run each experiment yourself before your students come to the laboratory. This practice is time consuming, but it will save you a great deal of difficulty in the long run. Once you have worked through the experiment yourself, you will know:

- exactly what equipment you will need for the day of the laboratory class
- how much time students should allow for each part of the experiment
- what material you can prepare as backups in case students fail to get the proper results in early stages of the experiment and their materials are unusable
- which parts of the experiment are most likely to cause problems for students and how to fix them
- what you should hope for in students' laboratory reports.

If it is impossible for you to run a laboratory experiment before the class meeting, carefully read the lab manual in advance and take note of the procedures or concepts that you cannot visualize without having run the experiment. Raise any questions you have during the preparatory session with the professor. Also, be sure to clarify these same points with your students; if it confused you, it will confuse them.

Laboratory Equipment

Prior to the first day of class, find time to go to the laboratory where you will be teaching. Make sure that you have the necessary access to the lab and to its materials. Check the equipment standard to the lab to see that it works. Even if the lab is in good working order, find out how to report equipment that needs to be repaired or replaced. For labs in which materials will be supplied on a weekly basis, find out who is responsible for maintaining and distributing the supplies and what teaching assistants are expected to do with regard to getting and returning supplies. Finally, locate the lab safety equipment (eye wash, fire extinguisher, etc.) and be sure that it is also in working order.

Laboratory Safety

Most laboratories involve a safety hazard of some kind. Be sure that you take time at the beginning of the semester to give your students clear instructions about the safety precautions of your laboratory. Once you have established the rules for safe laboratory procedures, enforce them vigilantly. If a student is being lax about safety (e.g., using a Bunsen burner for entertainment purposes) correct the student and alert them to the potential dangers of their behavior. If the student's dangerous behavior persists, you should—after appropriate warning—dismiss them from that particular lab and give them no credit for the lab or for the write-up.

Do not bend laboratory safety rules; if someone gets hurt under these circumstances, you will be held partly, if not fully, responsible. Be sure to lay out the laboratory safety rules and the consequences for breaking them in your syllabus. While it may feel like a hassle to send a student home when they show up wearing sandals or contact lenses to a chemistry laboratory that prohibits them, you are protecting the student and yourself by doing so.

Assigning Laboratory Groups

While some teaching assistants leave it to students to form their own groups, we recommend that you assign groups yourself according to these guidelines.

- Separate friends; this often helps students stay focused on the task at hand, and it reduces opportunities for lab report plagiarism.

- To the degree that it is possible, evenly divide the men and women in your class among the laboratory groups. As science students are often predominantly male, you may find that your female students have trouble asserting themselves as equal partners in their groups. If this is the case, you may want to consider creating some all-female groups.

- If you are aware that you have some students with more laboratory experience than others, you may want to pair them with less experienced students in order to ensure that most groups will finish the lab in a reasonable period of time. Make sure that the less experienced students are fully engaged and that the more experienced students are patient with them.

In extreme circumstances, students may need to switch lab groups. If such a situation arises, consult with the professor about how to approach the problem. You may be able to rearrange groups; you may have to move a student to another lab. Talk through with the professor how to present these changes to the students.

During the Laboratory

It is often effective to write an outline of the experiment steps on the board before class begins. When students arrive, talk them through the steps of the experiment and ask what questions they have about the procedure. Also, remind students of the aim of the lab and how it is relevant to lecture material. Once the experiment is under way, walk around the lab continuously and check in with each group. Students are far more likely to ask you important questions if you come to them than if you are sitting at a desk, away from the main activity of the lab. This also increases the energy level of the class and makes the whole thing more fun for everyone.

Answering Questions and Correcting Mistakes

When students have questions about the lab experiment, or when they are struggling with an experimental procedure, do not come to the rescue right away. Keep in mind that lab experiments are a vehicle through which students are taught about scientific methods and principles; it is far more important that your students understand the "big picture" behind a given experiment than that they achieve perfect experimental results. Student experiments have already been simplified and distilled to the level where they are manageable in a few hours. It can be important for students to see that experiments derail, that the next step is not always clear, and that decisions about how to proceed depend on the goal of the experiment.

Relate specific questions from your students to their broader understanding of the goals of the lab and ask them to make specific experimental decisions with this bigger picture in mind. Encourage students to work together to figure out an answer or how to get back on track with the experiment. Ask your students questions that will guide their thinking toward the information they need. Offer answers only when absolutely necessary.

EXAMPLE   "So, your bacteria didn't grow. Think of all the reasons why bacteria might not grow. Which ones might apply here?"

Keeping Students on Track and Involved

Experimental labs often involve periods of waiting between different phases of an experiment. You can use this time to engage students in question-and-answer periods designed to develop their understanding of the larger lesson behind any particular experiment. Ask your students questions that test their understanding of how the different parts of the lab experiment are related to the overall goals of the lab. You can also ask them questions about the lecture or present them with data or other information with which they have to generate a hypothesis. The point is to keep them immersed in the process of mastering the scientific method.

You are also likely to come across students who are happy to let their lab partners work on the experiment while they work on the crossword puzzle. This can be especially tricky when there really are more lab group members than tasks for particular parts of an experiment. Make a point of asking the crossword puzzler questions about the lab: what their partners are working on, the importance of this step in the experiment, and so on. Show students that you expect them to be fully involved in the lab and to understand what is happening, even if they have no specific task at that moment.

Wrapping Up the Lab

Because different lab groups will complete the experiment at different times, it is often impossible to give a final summary statement about the point of the lab. Instead, try to meet with each group of students as they are finishing to see how their experiment went and to answer questions they may have about how to summarize their findings in their lab reports. If necessary, you might want to institute a "formal" procedure in which groups are required to check in with you before leaving. This is also a good time to make sure that each lab group is cleaning up their equipment and returning their work space to its original condition.

Common Problems in Labs

It is unlikely that you will get through a single semester of teaching in a laboratory without facing at least one of the problems listed here.

Failed Experiments

For one reason or another, you will have a lab group whose experiment fails to achieve any semblance of the desired results. When this happens, remind your students that they can still do well on their lab reports. Instruct them to explain carefully why their experiment failed to achieve the expected results, to be frank about the shortcomings in their methods, and to take their experimental difficulties into account when interpreting any results they did achieve. Be sure to use failed experiments as a learning opportunity: ask students to generate hypotheses for their odd results and then describe how they would test these hypotheses to see what really went wrong. In this way a "failed" lab becomes another way to learn about the scientific method.

Students Who Miss Lab

Establish your policy on missed labs at the beginning of the semester and write it on the syllabus. Because it is nearly impossible to make up a missed lab, you need to be clear with your students about how you plan to handle absences.

Inattentive Students

While very inattentive students only hurt themselves in most classrooms, they can be a serious detriment to the safety of others in a laboratory. While you can expect an inattentive student's classmates to exert some pressure on the student to do their share, you should not place the burden of motivating an unmotivated student entirely on the other students in their group. You should address this kind of situation as early in the semester as possible.

Watch for students who are often (or always) reading the newspaper or chatting while the rest of their lab group is hard at work. During class, encourage the inattentive student to become involved in the work of the group.

> EXAMPLE "Maria, the rest of your group looks busy; find out from them what you should be doing."

You need to catch this kind of behavior as early as you can. Once a group of students identifies a member as "dead weight," they will often respond by isolating that student and figuring out how to work efficiently without them. At that point, it is more difficult for the student to be reintegrated into the group. If this behavior persists, schedule a meeting with the student outside of class to remind them of how their performance in the lab will affect their grade.

▣ Lab Reports

Once the lab is over, your students face the challenge of summarizing and explaining their results in a lab report. While students will learn to write better lab reports from trial and error, you can speed the learning process by offering some important information at the beginning of the term.

Explain the Purpose of Lab Reports

Students will often assume that you want them to mold their lab results—and their lab report—to what they think *should* have happened during the lab. Explain to students that experiments are as much about process as results. Tell students that it is possible to receive an A on a lab report summarizing a "failed" experiment and that students can also receive an F for a report on an experiment that went very well. What matters in the lab report is that students demonstrate their understanding of what was *supposed* to have happened in the lab, *why* it was supposed to have happened, and *how* their own results were achieved (even if their results are wrong!). Again, stress to your students that labs are designed to familiarize them with the scientific methods and principles of their field; the lab reports should be used to demonstrate their understanding of both.

Clarify Your Expectations

Tell your students in detail what format you prefer for lab reports: the necessary sections to include, how formal the writing should be, if reports may be handwritten, how many decimal places should be allowed for numerical results, if they may write their entire reports on graph paper, approximately how long a report should be, and so on. Describe explicitly what goes in each section of the report; it is a somewhat artificial way of organizing things, so students need a lot of guidance. Lab reports present a significant challenge to many students so take out as much of the guesswork about what you expect as you possibly can.

Also, be very clear with students (preferably on your course syllabus) about the penalties for late lab reports.

See pages 20–22 in Chapter 2, Syllabus: Setting the Agenda, for more information on establishing policies for the class.

Teach from Old Lab Reports

At the beginning of the term, make copies of old lab reports that students can use as models for their own reports (make sure they describe experiments your students will not be doing!). Review these reports with students and highlight the strengths and weaknesses of each report. Again, help your students to see the big picture behind lab experimentation and to appreciate how they can use their lab reports to communicate their understanding of how their results are related to the goals of the lab. Talk with students about *why* lab reports are set up according to a particular format, why all the included information is important for them as scientists.

Group Lab Reports

There are benefits and drawbacks to asking students to write group lab reports.

PROS   Students learn more about working in groups.

It involves less grading for you.

Students can pool their knowledge.

CONS   It may be difficult to ascertain the understanding of individual group members.

It may discourage active lab participation by all members of the group.

Some students may do almost no work, while others will do the lion's share.

See pages 139–40 in Chapter 7, Grading Group Work, for more information on how to grade group assignments.

You may want to alternate assignments, asking students to write some lab reports individually and some in groups.

Teach from New Lab Reports

Each week, you can ask one group to prepare a presentation for the next lab in which they give an oral lab report (with a much reduced Methods section). This allows the class as a whole to sum up the previous lab and discuss problems or theoretical issues. It also keeps students from forgetting (quite so immediately!) what they did the previous week.

▣ Developing Essay Assignments

A good essay assignment takes time and thought to develop. While there can sometimes be value to giving students a more open-ended essay prompt (e.g., "Write a 10-page research paper on a topic of your choosing related to the course theme"), students will typically produce better essays with a more specific prompt that provides clarity about the genre of the essay and that helps steer them toward good topics.

The Prompt

The prompt for an essay assignment will often range from one to a few detailed paragraphs. The content of those paragraphs is described. Don't overwhelm students with too much information; think about what material is required on the prompt and what you can discuss in class. Also, don't leave students adrift with a prompt that does not specify genre, topic, and format requirements.

As a teaching assistant, you may not craft the prompts for course essays. However, you can help students work with the prompt successfully by guiding them through the process of writing the essay.

Genre Expectations

Figure out what genre of essay you are asking students to write (persuasive, descriptive, informative, narrative, etc.) and specify that in the prompt. Most of these genres will make an academic argument, and it can help to remind students of the importance of having a central argument in the prompt itself.

If possible, provide students with models of essays written in that genre. The models may be published essays or student work from previous terms.

Selecting Topics

Students will typically produce the strongest writing when they are writing about topics they care about. When possible, give them some choice in topics. There are a couple of ways to do this. The prompt can list a set of questions, allowing students to choose among them. The prompt can also lay down very specific parameters but leave the topic open: for example, a critical media analysis of an advertising campaign of the student's choosing, a definitional argument about a word of the student's choosing, or a description of a selected cultural ritual. One key component of the latter strategy is that students can feel like they have the genuine opportunity to write something original, to share with you and their peers information that you did not know.

Specifying Format

Be clear in the prompt about the formal requirements of the essay. If you expect students to use appropriate outside sources, tell them so; if you do not, let students know. If the essay should have a coherent argument/thesis, remind students in the prompt (students sometimes believe that factual papers do not need an argument). If students can be creative in responding to the prompt, acknowledge that possibility explicitly. If you are looking for a good title and/or an engaging first sentence, be clear about that too.

Specify the expected length of the essay and any other parameters about spacing, margins, etc. With essay length, it can be useful to indicate how many words the essay should be (e.g., approximately 3,000 words), which avoids the issue of students using larger fonts to fill space, for example. If you choose to use page length requirements, think carefully about specifications such as "a 4–6 page essay": a four-page essay and a six-page essay involve significantly different responses to a prompt; if are you looking for an approximately five-page essay, simply say that.

Process

If possible, help students with writing the essay by breaking the process into steps. Talk specifically with your students about the steps involved in writing a successful essay: moving from a topic or question to research/development of the topic, articulating a preliminary argument, drafting the essay, refining the argument, revising the essay, etc. Students often think that they will know their argument from the get-go, but we know that it actually takes a lot of preliminary work to develop good arguments. Breaking the process of essay writing into steps reinforces that message for students. Requiring steps in the process can allow you to head off an unpromising topic in its early stages, while a student still has time to take another path.

Here are some ways to implement some of the steps in class:

- Students email you with their proposed question for investigation and a brief description of how they propose to begin their investigation. (Consider whether you want them to email you with "an argument" at this early stage, as opposed to a question or a hypothesis, given that they have not had time to do research or develop their ideas.)

- Students bring a short proposal for their essay to class. In small groups, they workshop these proposals with their peers, guided by some questions from you.

- Students participate in a workshop of essay drafts.

> See pages 93–98 in Chapter 5, Essay Workshop, for more information about how to run a workshop.

When you first introduce the essay prompt, talk with students about how you would go about approaching the essay and what you might write about. As a class, brainstorm possible topics or ask students who know what they want to write about to share those ideas with the class.

Questions to Ask Yourself

Once you have drafted an essay assignment, ask someone else to read it and let you know if anything is unclear. Also, ask yourself these questions:

- Could I write an essay of this length in the allotted time?
- Do I want to read these essays?

If the answer to either question is no, then you need to rewrite the prompt. If you couldn't write the essay, it is not fair to expect your students to do so. If you don't want to read the essays, all odds are that your students will not be excited about writing them. Go back and try to create a prompt that allows students to write original, interesting essays.

▣ Creating Exams

As a teaching assistant you may have limited opportunities to write course exams as this duty often falls to the course professor. However, should the opportunity arise for you to develop an exam, test, or quiz, consider the following guidelines in approaching the task.

Focus on Learning Objectives

Ideally, the course you teach should be organized around a series of learning objectives. As noted in Chapter 5, learning objectives focus on the new content or the new skills students should master by the end of the course. As a teaching assistant, you may have little say in shaping the learning objectives for the course and/or you may be assisting an instructor who does not articulate clear learning objectives for students. All the same, you will create successful exams if you begin by articulating the learning objectives the exam is designed to assess. To do so, you may want to return to the course syllabus, your lesson plans, recent reading or written assignments, and so on.

Think Outside the Box

It is easy to fall into the habit of giving students the same kinds of assessments we received as students ourselves without considering whether or not these assessments effectively measure student mastery of the course learning objectives. For example, multiple choice questions are easy to grade, but a poorly designed multiple choice test may assess only a student's superficial understanding of course material and not one's ability to apply what was learned to new problems. Similarly, straightforward passage identification tests—a favorite in English departments—often test whether or not the student read and remembered the texts while failing to measure other important factors such as the student's understanding of the passage's meaning, relevance, or literary properties. As you can see, if you step back, review the course learning objectives, and put them at the center of creating the exam, you will discover that some tried-and-true testing techniques will not meet your needs.

To effectively assess student mastery of the course learning objectives, develop questions that target specific skill or knowledge demonstration. You may be able to employ multiple choice or short answer questions to achieve this; you may need to ask students to solve problems longhand or write narrative responses.

EXAMPLE   *Learning objective:* Students should be able to analyze novel data by applying the appropriate statistical equation.

Sample assessment question: Using the data provided, select and apply the formula that will allow you to determine whether there is a statistical significance between the two groups. Explain why you selected that formula.

You may discover that to assess some learning objectives, you need to be creative. Very smart, challenging questions can involve accessible, sometimes funny scenarios or problems. Don't hesitate to make your exam as intellectually interesting—and even entertaining—an experience as possible.

EXAMPLE   *Learning objective:* Students should be able to
effectively describe course concepts to someone
who is unfamiliar with the material.

Sample assessment question: The parents of a good
friend of yours are criticizing the way that young
people speak, with lots of *like, you know, I mean,
dude, well.* "Useless clutter," they say about these
words. Make a persuasive argument to these parents that these forms are not always useless clutter.

Thinking Ahead about Grading

You will be happier as you grade the exam if you have thought
about grading criteria while writing the exam. This is particularly
important with short answer, problem solving, or essay questions.
For example, with short answer questions, determine what constitutes a complete response (and alert students to this criterion) and
whether you will give partial credit. With problem-solving questions, specify whether students need to show their work and
whether partial credit is available if the final answer is incorrect.
With essay questions, decide whether it needs to be a full essay or
a detailed paragraph. Limiting the length of the response can save
you from grading "buckshot" essays in which students write everything they know in hopes that something they write will hit the
target.

EXAMPLE   *Learning objective:* Students should be able to
summarize the major factors that led to the
Gulf War.

Sample assessment question: List
three economic forces that contributed to the Gulf War and
provide a detailed paragraph
explaining how they intersected
with military interests.

See pages 88–91 in Chapter
5, Exam Preparation, for
information on how to use
class time to prepare for an
exam. See pages 124–26 in
Chapter 7, Grading Exams, for
more information about
grading strategies.

Further Reading

Clarke, J., and A. Biddle, eds. 1993. *Teaching Critical Thinking: Reports from across the Curriculum.* Englewood Cliffs, NJ: Prentice Hall.

Davidson, N., ed. 1990. *Cooperative Learning in Mathematics: A Handbook for Teachers.* Menlo Park, CA: Addison-Wesley.

Seymour, E. 2000. *Talking about Leaving: Why Undergraduates Leave the Sciences.* Boulder, CO: Westview Press.

Svinicki, M., and W. J. McKeachie. 2011. *McKeachie's Teaching Tips: Strategies, Research, and Theory for College and University Teachers.* 13th ed. Belmont, CA: Wadsworth.

Tobias, S. 1992. *Revitalizing Undergraduate Science: Why Some Things Work and Most Things Don't.* Tucson, AZ: Research Corp.

Grading

Grading is one of the most difficult and arguably the least enjoyable parts of teaching. Teaching assistants often spend too much time grading their students' work and worrying about it afterward. This chapter is designed to help you make the grading process more efficient, less stressful, and more fair to you and your students.

■ Grade Calculations

At the beginning of the term, you will want to determine the point values of all assignments and decide how those point totals will convert into a final grade. If you prefer to give letter grades rather than point grades on assignments, be sure to determine a point value for each letter grade (e.g., A+ = 100, A = 95, A– = 90, etc.) so that you have a basis for calculating final grades at the end of the term. At the beginning of the semester, let your students know how their final grade will be calculated; having a transparent grading system gives students a clear sense of where they stand in your course and helps you to be fair and accurate when assigning final grades.

If you plan to use a check/check plus/check minus system for more informal work, think ahead about how these scores will translate into a final grade for that part of the course. The same holds true if you are grading participation.

> See Appendix A for a detailed example of point values for assignments and how those points convert to a final grade.

Grade Books

When to Make a Grade Book

Wait about two weeks after classes begin before you create your permanent grade book; by then, most students have finished dropping and adding courses from their schedules. For the first two weeks, keep track of absences (and early grades, if applicable) on the attendance sheets provided by the department, in a temporary grade book, or by passing around an attendance sheet at the beginning of each class. You can usually acquire a grade book from your department or from a local bookstore.

How to Organize a Grade Book

Leave yourself plenty of space in the grade book in case you need to add revised grades, notes, or grade subtotals. It is easiest and clearest if you record absences and grades in different places. If the grade book has internal flaps, you can record grades on one flap and absences on another while using the same list of student names. Alphabetical order for students' names is a sure bet.

In recording absences, be sure to mark the date of absences in case students question their attendance or the participation part of the final grade. Also record late arrivals if a certain number of them is equivalent to an absence.

In recording graded material, set up columns for different kinds of assignments: papers, lab reports, problem sets, daily homework assignments, exams. Within each larger column, label individual columns for each assignment or exam. By grouping similar assignments in the grade book, you can more easily tally subtotals of the final grade and calculate their percentage of the final grade. In later sections of the grade book, you can reduplicate the class list and keep notes about students' progress, difficulties, successes, participation, and so on. These notes can be helpful at the end of the term in grading participation and in writing letters of recommendation.

Using Electronic Grade Books

Spreadsheet computer programs such as Excel or Claris make computing final grades a snap. The initial programming (e.g., creating the percentage values of each column) can take time, but at the end of the term, once all the grades are entered, the computer does all the math and does it accurately. If you use such a program, set up your columns exactly as you would in a traditional grade book.

Do not necessarily abandon the traditional grade book if you choose to use a computer program. Computers crash; programs (or you!) delete data. In addition, you can carry your grade book with you to record absences during class or assignment grades if you are grading somewhere other than next to your computer.

Preserving Your Records

Your grade book is a critical item, and its loss would be unpleasant for you and your students. To protect yourself and the grades, make photocopies of the grade book every couple of weeks so that you have backup records. If you're using a computer program, regularly back up and print out the records.

Once the term is over, keep the grade book at least two terms, if not longer. You will need these records if a student questions a grade. And these records can prove invaluable if a student later asks for a letter of recommendation.

Grading Exams

Exams can be some of the easiest material to grade because you (should) have a clear idea of your expectations and because all of your students are answering the same questions. When you sit down to grade a stack of exams, you should have a key to the exam that details the correct (or acceptable) answers and point values for each question. Ideally, you (or your professor) should write this key when you design the exam—this will help ensure that you have a good exam and that your questions have clear right answers (and no typos!).

Grading Logistics

Here are some hints that will save you time and answer many of your students' post-exam questions.

- Every time you subtract points for an answer, write the number of points you are taking off next to the answer.

- Total the number of points taken off in each section or page and circle that total in the margin.

- Then, when you are calculating the final score, you can simply add the negative subtotals (which will be circled) for each section.

- Write, in brief, the correct answer next to the question when you take off points. You do not need to do this if you will review the exam in detail during class, if you will put an answer key on the course website, or if the student made no attempt to answer the question.

- If you find yourself writing more on the student's exam than the student did, *stop!* Determine the final score, put the score at the top of the exam, and write next to it "Come see me" or the equivalent. Then arrange a meeting with this student to find out what happened on the exam.

Grading Right/Wrong Questions

Questions that have right or wrong answers (multiple choice, fill in the blank, matching, etc.) are a cinch to grade as long as you know the point value for each question. If you are not going to review these in class, you should write the correct answer next to each missed question, hand out a copy of the key, or post a copy of the key on the course website.

Grading Short Answer Questions

Most short answer sections involve partial credit. You need to break down the answer and decide how much each part is worth. When you are grading, you can then subtract the given number of points for each part of the answer that is not included. Next to the subtraction, write (in a word or two) the idea that the student missed.

Grading Essay Questions on Exams

Grading essay questions on an exam can be a longer version of grading short answer questions. There are, however, some differences. First, decide what major points a student needs to include, how much each point is worth, and how much development of the idea you expect. Next, for each major point, decide how much credit you will give for partially developed answers and vague allusions to the idea in question. You may want to put a check mark next to each significant essay point as you grade.

If you let them, some students will write everything they know that might have anything to do with the correct answer to the question. To avoid this, when you hand out the exam, tell your students that you are aware of this exam-taking strategy. You may even confess to having used this technique yourself. Tell them that such answers are not suitable and that they should be sure to answer the exam question as it is posed to them. Tell students how short their answers can be: if you know that the correct answer only requires a couple of informed paragraphs, for example, tell them. Having said all this, you are not obligated to give full credit for run-on, buckshot essays.

Adjusting Class Scores

When you grade an exam, be attentive to questions that a great majority of students miss. If you come across one of these, look at the question again to be sure that it is fair. If it is not a fair question, consider dropping it from the exam or lowering its weight in the exam grade.

If all of the scores on an exam are low, the first thing to ask yourself is whether the problem is with the exam or with the students. If it is a problem with the exam, you may need to drop problematic sections from the total score or curve the overall score.

If the problem is with the students (you can usually tell that this is the case if a few students do well on the exam), do not feel you need to adjust the scores. Remember that low scores on tests before the final exam can provide motivation for students to work harder. What you do need to do is speak frankly with your students about their performance.

See pages 141–42 in this chapter, Handing Back Graded Material, for more information on what to say when handing back exams with many low scores.

Grading Essays

Some students will complain that essay grades are subjective and, of course, they are to some extent right. But there are some objective standards of good writing. The clearer you can make these standards to yourself and to your students, the easier your grading will be. If possible, with an essay assignment, provide students with a rubric of the criteria for essay grades. Write these criteria carefully because they will become the reference point for you and your students.

An A Paper: A paper that is exceptional. It is interesting or unusual and demonstrates sophistication of thought. The main argument and the supporting points are clear, complex, and well developed. The structure of the paper follows a clear, logical organization, and all sources are critically examined. It is free of grammatical and spelling errors.

A B Paper: A paper that is solid and fulfills the assignment. It has a clear argument but minor lapses in development. It touches on the complexity of the argument and shows careful reading of the sources. The structure follows a logical progression of ideas, but not all evidence is clearly related to the main ideas. It may contain a few grammatical usage problems but not enough to make reading difficult.

A C Paper: A paper that is adequate but less effective in responding to the assignment. It presents the central idea in general terms and demonstrates basic comprehension of the sources. It is difficult to find a logical structure to the argument, and the paper often relies on generalizations or on unrelated examples. Sentences may be awkward or confusing enough to make reading difficult.

A D Paper: A paper that does not have a clear argument or does not respond to the assignment. The argument may be too vague or obvious to be developed, and there is little complexity in the ideas. The organization can be difficult to follow, and the paper offers insufficient evidence.

An F Paper: A paper that does not respond to the assignment, has no central argument, and uses no sources. There is little apparent organization. There is no supporting evidence, or it is irrelevant.

Keeping Control of Grading Time

Grading papers can suck up as much time as you let it. You should not spend more than 20 to 30 minutes grading the standard undergraduate paper (four to seven pages). You are not doing yourself or the student any favors if you take more time than this. Keep a watch nearby, and force yourself to check how long each paper is taking you. Make yourself speed up if you are taking more than half an hour per paper.

Taking less time will mean making fewer comments, but students cannot necessarily distinguish between the important and less important points in an extended barrage of comments. Concisely point out the next step the student should take in the improvement of their writing, leaving later steps for your comments on the next assignment.

For example, if a paper is riddled with spelling and usage errors, the main argument is unclear, and the student misunderstood some of the sources, do not aim to comment on all of these problems. Begin by addressing the most fundamental problems—in this case perhaps the coherence of the argument. Then you can point out one major usage problem and tell the student you expect them to use the spell checker. In your comments on the next paper, you can then address the student's progress with these aspects of the paper and move on to the next step in improving the writing, perhaps the use of secondary material. It will help you to keep a summary of these comments in your grade book so that you can remember from paper to paper where students have been having difficulties. Alternately, you can ask students to attach previous papers and/or drafts (with your comments) when handing in their most recent assignment.

Choosing Electronic or Paper Grading

It's up to you whether you want to grade electronic or paper versions of student essays (unless the course professor has an established policy). In making that decision, here are a few things to consider.

Electronic Grading

PROS   Some instructors find it faster to type comments into the text using comment bubbles and Track Changes.

You have an electronic record of all student work and your comments.

Carrying around your laptop is easier than hauling around a stack of 40 papers, and you can't lose the papers.

CONS   Some instructors find it slower to type comments into the text using comment bubbles and Track Changes, and they lose the ability to flip pages to find specific parts of the text.

A technical glitch could cause you to lose a lot of work you've done.

Paper Grading

PROS   Handwritten comments can seem more personal than typed comments.

You can grade paper copies anywhere—you don't need a computer, Internet access, or an outlet.

Some instructors find it faster to comment by hand.

CONS   You have no record of student papers or your comments unless you make copies of all graded student work.

If you have illegible handwriting, students may line up outside your door to have you read your comments to them (or ignore your comments because they cannot read them).

Handwritten comments make it harder to go back and revise your own comments and can look sloppy.

If you choose to grade hard copies of students' essays you may want to avoid red pens for grading unless you have a particular fetish for that color. Red ink carries a lot of baggage for most students, and they will be more receptive to your comments if they are not in red ink. Purple and green pens work nicely because the colors are dark enough to keep the writing legible; blue pens also can work if you are writing on typed essays. Using a pencil is problematic because the lead smears over time and students can, if they are so inspired, change the grade or erase your comments. You do not want to run the risk of having a student alter a grade written in pencil and then approach you at the end of the term about a "miscalculation" in their grade.

Moving Out of Problem-Solving Mode

Problem solving is one of the biggest temptations and biggest traps in paper grading. When you read an essay that has, for example, serious organizational problems, your first reaction may be to figure out how to reorganize the essay so that it makes sense. This is not your job; it is the student's job. You can waste an enormous amount of time doing their work. Instead, you should tell them that the organization is weak and point out where and why. Ask questions; let them figure out the answers and how to fix the essay.

DON'T   "The organization of the argument is hard to follow. You talk first about X and then about Y. You then jump to Z. But X and Z are related, so why not talk about them together? It might work well to start with Y because it could tie in with your introduction. Z is clearly your strongest point, so perhaps you want to lead up to that. Then you could use the conclusion to tie back to the introduction. . . ."

DO   "The organization of the argument is hard to follow. You talk first about X and then about Y. You then jump to Z. Is there a logic to this ordering? Which ideas are related, and which are most important?"

DON'T   "In your argument for legalizing marijuana, you do not address the arguments against legalization. Many people would argue that legalizing marijuana will lead to greater use and to less concern about possible health risks. People may also stop making a distinction between cigarettes and pot. . . ."

Do   "In your argument for legalizing marijuana, you need to address the arguments on the other side of the issue. What points do people make in favor of keeping the present laws? How can you counter these? And what is the most effective way to organize these points and counterpoints when you revise this paper?"

Giving Feedback throughout the Paper

Begin by skimming through the paper to see the argument and get a sense of the organization (or lack thereof). Next, read the paper carefully with your pen in hand, commenting on ideas and marking specifically targeted areas of the writing. If you are going to grade several papers over the course of the term and you like to use abbreviated editing marks when you grade, provide students with a key at the beginning of the term so that they can understand what you have written on their papers.

	A Guide to the Cryptic Marks on Your Papers
℈	This word, space, or letter should be deleted.
¶	A new paragraph should begin here.
WC	Word Choice: Another word would be clearer or more effective here.
frag	This is a sentence fragment.
sp	Spelling: This word is misspelled.
a	Capitalize this letter.
#	You need a space here.
quo\status/	These two words should be in the reverse order.
some one	This is one word.

Comments on Ideas

The margins are the ideal place to comment on smaller ideas within a paper because you will not have the time or space to mention them in the final comments. If a student makes a particularly good or specious argument, write a note there. If the student makes a confusing point, ask a question there.

Comments on Usage and Style

You cannot comment on everything, so try to be thematic. If the student is having problems with sentence fragments, mark those and do not try to mark all the sections that are consequently choppy. Focus on fixing one significant problem at a time.

If you are factoring grammar into the paper grade, seriously consider how much weight it should carry compared to the content of the work. Be especially careful about grading students harshly for usage "problems" that are debatable (e.g., split infinitives, ending a sentence with a preposition, singular generic *they*). And remember that a student's style and/or dialect may be very different from your own. At the same time, it is true that unclear usage can undermine the quality of students' writing; use your comments to show them how they might construct sentences more effectively. Along these lines, consider substituting words like "effective" and "ineffective" for "right" and "wrong" in many circumstances.

Comments on Spelling and Typographical Errors

Do not waste time correcting spelling errors and typos. You can choose to circle them as you see them, but you do not have to fix them. If these kinds of mistakes are particularly pervasive in a given essay, make a general comment on the need to proofread and, if appropriate, dock the grade for these mistakes. Students may not see the importance of ridding their papers of "little" mistakes unless they are penalized for them. You can explain to them that their readers may have trouble taking their argument seriously if it is presented sloppily.

Positive Comments

Do not write only negative comments or questions in the margins. If a sentence or paragraph is particularly well written, say so. If an argument is strong or well presented, say so. Students can learn as much from what they do successfully as from what they do unsuccessfully.

Feedback on the Whole Essay

The final comments are the time to address the global aspects of the essay. Tackle the big things like the essay's argument, the organization, the major supporting arguments or facts, and the overall writing style. Leave the smaller points for the marginal notes. And remember that you do not have to solve the problems—your job is to point them out.

Scope

The key to writing good comments on students' work is striking the balance between too little and too much. Bear in mind how frustrated you have been over the years when you have put time into an assignment only to get it back with a grade and nothing else on the last page. Of equal importance, remember that students can absorb only so much constructive criticism in one shot. Focus your comments on one or two major issues and perhaps one minor one (e.g., the style of the conclusion) and accept the fact that you cannot cover all the bases in your response to one assignment.

Form

For shorter assignments, writing your comments in the margins and on the last page often works well. For extended essays, teaching assistants generally opt to write a longer set of comments either on the last page or on a separate page stapled to the essay. For these longer sets of comments, it is helpful and kind (if a bit cliché) to follow the "Positive comment but Negative—yet constructive—comment" formula.

> EXAMPLE   "You set up the essay beautifully with the story in the beginning, and the conclusion nicely circles back to that story. But the organization of the paragraphs in between is not always clear. . . ."

Or you can use the first sentence to summarize the student's argument before you discuss its strengths and weaknesses. We recommend starting the comments by addressing the student directly and ending them by signing your name.

EXAMPLE   "Sarah,

> You have chosen a provocative topic, and you clearly recognize the importance of including both sides of the issue. The next step is to think about how you want to organize these ideas. . . . I look forward to reading the next draft.
>
> Jackie"

Legibility

In your comments, legibility is critical. It is incredibly frustrating for students if they cannot read your writing; if you do not write legibly, you might as well not write the comments at all.

If you choose to type your comments, be careful: some teaching assistants have found that their comments sound or become harsher when they type them, perhaps because they adopt the critical mind-set of their own academic work in front of the computer or, perhaps, simply because typed comments look and feel more impersonal. The advantage of typed comments is that you automatically have a record of your comments on all students' work.

Monitoring Student Progress

You may want to keep notes on your own comments so that you can cover different issues on each assignment. You can use pages in the back of your grade book for notes about each student, or you can keep them in a running computer file. You can also ask students to keep their papers and hand in all of the work they have done in your class with each new paper or at the end of the semester. Some teaching assistants warn students about their impending doom if they force the teaching assistant to comment on the same problem twice, but you should remember that the "same" problem can be difficult to define and a student's concerted effort to work on a problem may not be entirely successful.

Finding Your Grading Curve

You have to find the "zone" of grades that makes you feel comfortable and that is acceptable at your university. You want to be sure that you feel comfortable with the grades you give so that you can justify them to your students if you have to. That does not mean giving higher grades; it means understanding what you are conveying through each grade and what the student needs to do to get a higher grade.

Grading gets easier over time as you read more and more undergraduate papers. You acquire a better sense of the range of undergraduate writing and where a given paper falls in that range. And as you get more comfortable with grading, you will feel more confident about the grades that you assign.

Until you gain that confidence, there are strategies you can use to reassure yourself that each student receives the grade they have earned. It is usually easy to know how the papers in a class compare to each other, from the best to the worst. The hard part is knowing what grade that means each paper should get. Grading criteria can provide you with the guidelines and justifications for assigning particular grades. Obviously, if you feel comfortable assigning grades on papers as you go, this is an efficient and usually effectively accurate way to grade. If you are not yet at that point, you can try one of these strategies.

Strategy 1

Comment on the papers completely, but do not put a grade on them. As you finish each paper, arrange it in the stack of graded papers from best to worst. When you finish all the papers, decide which papers (if any) deserve an A, which (if any) deserve an F, and where the rest fall in between. You will find that these decisions correspond to your criteria and that your grades are consistent.

Strategy 2

Comment on the papers completely, and write the grade for each on a separate sheet of paper. You then have the flexibility to change a grade or the overall curve if you realize that you started out too low or too high. Once you are finished grading, go back and write each grade on the corresponding paper.

Allowing Revision

Students can learn a great deal from revising their papers, and it can provide your comments on a paper with a direct and immediate purpose. But grading all the revised versions can take a huge amount of your time. Here are a few suggestions.

- Set a limit on the number of papers a student can revise during the term.

- Set a time limit (e.g., two weeks) after you return a set of papers for accepting revised versions. This way, students must be organized and motivated to rewrite the paper; they cannot revise all their papers at the end of the term in a last-ditch effort to raise their grade.

- Warn students that their grades can go down as well as up on a revised paper.

- Establish guidelines for what constitutes "revision"; otherwise students may simply correct the punctuation and turn the paper back in.

- Ask students to turn in the original paper with the revision so that you can compare the two.

▨ Grading Problem Sets

The first key to facilitating problem set grading is designing the assignment to be easy to grade. The goal of the entire assignment and of its parts should be clear enough that students know what is expected and you know what you are expecting.

Setting Guidelines for Students

Tell students explicitly how you want the problem sets formatted. You may want to provide examples on the board or on a handout. Some features to specify:

- whether the assignment should be typed or neatly written (in pen or in pencil)

- how big/small students can write and how much space they should leave

- how they should identify the answer (circling it, etc.)

- how much explanation they should provide for steps within the problem (e.g., identify the theorem by name or spell it out)

- your policy on legibility (e.g., if you cannot read it, you will not grade it), decimal places expected, format, and level of detail.

Setting Point Values

Decide how many points each assignment is worth and how those points are assigned to the problems. Then determine how you will grade each problem by assigning the amount of credit students will receive for:

- the right answer

- the correct stages/methodology to move toward the answer

- legibility.

Effort is clearly a subjective basis for grading, and if problem sets are not a major grade, you may choose not to use this as a criterion, or you may incorporate it as part of having the correct stages laid out in a problem. Explain to students how you assign point values at the beginning of the term or before a given assignment if the system changes for various assignments.

> See page 101 in Chapter 6, Framing the Assessment of Problem Sets, for more information on establishing expectations for problem sets.

Logistics of Grading Problem Sets

Subtract points for each problem as you go. For obvious errors, circle the problem and write the point subtraction next to it. If you are taking off additional subjective points, write a short one-sentence or one-phrase comment to explain the error.

> See pages 139–40 in this chapter, Grading Group Work, for more information on grading problem sets completed by groups of students.

▣ Grading Lab Reports

√ Setting Guidelines for Students

Lab reports will be easier for you to grade if your students understand your expectations for the content and format of the report.

> See pages 113–15 in Chapter 6, Lab Reports, for more information on introducing lab reports.

√ Setting Point Values

Subdivide the points for each lab report as much as possible. This allows you to give credit for each part of the report the student completes correctly. Obviously, you will want to weight point values toward the interpretive sections of the lab report.

√ Logistics of Grading Lab Reports

Briefly read through all or at least several of the lab reports to determine how students did overall and where you may encounter problems. Once you begin grading, score each section of the lab report separately so that students see their strengths and weaknesses in the presentation of the results. Write the score for each section in the margin; you can then quickly calculate the overall grade at the end. Some advice for grading the different parts of lab reports follows.

Grading Descriptive Sections

For sections that address equipment, methods, and other standardized aspects of the lab, you can easily subtract points for missing information. Unless you will review the lab reports in class, briefly note what the students missed.

Grading Results

You need to decide how much it matters in the final lab report that the students achieve the results expected from the experiment. Remember, students with little understanding may get perfect results, while students with near-complete understanding may come up with the wrong results.

Grading Interpretive Sections

Interpretive sections (e.g., discussion of results, conclusions) require a combination of objective and subjective grading. Determine how much credit you will give for the correct answer(s). Then give yourself a range of points to award for the degree to which a student communicates their understanding of how the results relate to the broader goals of the experiment (this is where students can get credit for effort). If you subtract points for lack of understanding, do not feel compelled to explain the problem in depth in the margins; instead, write a question in the margin that directs the student toward the information they missed.

Grading Troublesome Sections

Occasionally, the whole class will struggle in the write-up of one section of the experiment. When grading these sections, you may want to lower your expectations and grade more leniently. Then, if possible, review this section in class with all the students.

Grading Group Work

There are two general philosophies about grading group work: one grade for the entire group or different grades for each group member based on effort. Some instructors love group work. Other instructors feel that group work allows lazy students to ride on the coattails of their hard-working peers.

Each student in the group receives the same grade.

PROS It is the easiest way to assign grades for group work.

It can encourage students to make the most of working as a group.

A combined grade reflects the "real world" consequences of a group effort: it is the final product, not the contributions of each group member, that counts.

CONS Some students will put in more work than others, but they all will receive the same grade.

Each student's grade is based on individual contribution to the group project.

PROS   Some students will put in more work than others, and their grades will be higher.

It can encourage students to work equally hard.

CONS   It can foster tension between group members because they are asked to judge each other's effort.

It is a more time-consuming way of assigning grades.

Assigning Grades Based on Individual Effort

1. Determine an overall grade for the project.

2. Ask each student to turn in a list of the group members and their perception of the percentage of effort put into the project by each member. Remind students that the percentages should add up to 100 percent.

3. Average the percentages for each student.

4. Adjust each student's grade according to the percentage of work they contributed to the project. To do this, multiply the final grade (give it a number value) by the number of students working on the project. Then for each student, multiply that number by the percentage of effort they contributed. Convert these numbers back to letter grades if necessary.

EXAMPLES   Overall project grade = B (3.0)

3.0×4 students = 12

All students about Student 1: 25 percent, 25 percent, 30 percent, 20 percent = 25 percent (make this calculation for each student)

Student 1: 25 percent $\times$ 12 = 3.0 (B)

Student 2: 25 percent $\times$ 12 = 3.0 (B)

Student 3: 35 percent $\times$ 12 = 4.2 (A or A+)

Student 4: 15 percent $\times$ 12 = 1.8 (C–)

▣ Handing Back Graded Material

Each student's grades are between you and that student only. Never hand back graded material in a way that will compromise any student's confidentiality with regard to their grade (e.g., if you have arranged papers in order by grade, do not hand them back that way). For longer papers, put the grade on the last page with your comments or staple your typed comments to the back of the paper; you then can have students pass the papers to each other. For one-page assignments or exams with a grade on the top, be prepared to walk around the classroom and hand back the material to students individually or put the grade on the back of the assignment.

Handing Back Papers

Unless you intend to spend class time making general comments about papers, hand them back at the end of class. If you start by giving students their papers, they will read through your comments instead of paying attention, and students who got low grades may choose not to participate in class because they feel disheartened or because they wish to express a form of protest. Tell students at the beginning of class that you will be handing back papers at the end so that they do not leave early.

Prepare students for the grades. If the grades are generally low, tell students this, explaining why and where many students had trouble. Explain the weight of this paper and what students can do to improve their grades. If you were disappointed with the papers, tell them so. If you were pleased, tell them so. Positive reinforcement can do wonders for class morale, and it can motivate students who realize their grades are falling below the class standard.

Positive and negative feedback to the entire class can motivate both stronger and weaker students, and it gives them some sense of where their grade fits into the range of grades in the class. Students also find it helpful to have some class or section statistics (e.g., mean, standard deviation, etc.) if they can be made available. Always remind students how they can reach you if they want to talk about their papers more than is possible during class.

Handing Back Exams

As with papers, unless you intend to spend class time reviewing the exams, hand them back at the end of class. Tell students the class average or range of grades so they know where they stand. If you are not running a review, briefly explain how you graded the exam and how students can reach you if they have questions.

Possible Climate Changes

Returning the first graded assignment can be like the "end of the romance." Assigning grades can sometimes mark a shift in how your students perceive you and the class. Some of them may have seen you as a friend or ally, and it can be jolting for them to be reminded that you give the grades and they get them. If there is a mood swing in the class with the first set of grades, it is almost always temporary—students rebound and remember that there are many assignments over the term and that the grading criteria are objective standards, not personal ones. Remember that the students are not disappointed in or angry at you; they are more often disappointed in their own performance. Keeping this in mind, do not feel that you need to apologize or to cater to their wishes for high grades or for a "teacher friend"; but do make it clear how they can improve their performance and how you can facilitate that.

In preparing your lesson plans, you may want to make sure that your classes that day and the next involve a high level of student participation so that students continue to feel invested in the success of the class.

"In trying to explain to students how grades measure mastery rather than simply reward effort, I talk about the football team. I remind them that lots of players go to practice every single day and often practice even harder than the starting players, but they understand that this does not necessarily mean that they will get to start."

In-Class Review of Exams

There are times when you should devote part of a class period to reviewing exams because your feedback will apply to all the students. Reviewing an exam is a form of teaching: you will be reviewing or clarifying material that should be (but clearly isn't!) familiar to your students. Also, reviewing an exam in class can ease the work of grading: you only need to subtract points and not provide reasons on the exam itself.

When to Begin the Review

Unless you intend to spend the whole class period on exam review, you should always do an exam review toward the end of class. Once you hand back exams, students will be distracted and unable to focus on any other agenda. Decide how much time you will need to address the biggest problem areas of the exam and set aside that much time at the end of class.

Ending the Review

Another benefit of reviewing the exam near the end of class is that you have a clear-cut end to the discussion. If the class period ends before you have had the chance to address important questions brought up by your students, you can take more time to go over the exam during the next class meeting. If you have a few students with very specific questions, invite them to your office hours for a more tailored exam review.

How to Run the Review

After grading the exams, you will have a sense of the areas where students had trouble. You may want to begin the review by identifying the sections where most students did not have problems. Tell your class that you do not have time to review these sections but that, if they have questions, they should come talk to you after class or during office hours.

Take the section of the exam that gave students the most trouble and tell the students that many of them struggled with this section. You then can ask, "What do you think it is about this section that made it so hard for you?" This will get the discussion started.

Let the students help each other get the right answers. Moderate the discussion so that students listen to each other and do not get sidetracked.

Do not suggest to your students that they are dumb.

DON'T   "Other students have not had trouble with this exam in the past—there is no good reason why you all should have performed so poorly."

DO   "I was surprised by the low scores. What do you think went wrong?"

"How did you study for this exam? What might change in your approach to studying next time?"

"Do you have thoughts about what we can do in class to make you feel more prepared for the next exam?"

Do more than just give out the answers.

DON'T   "Number one. The right answer is X. Number two . . ."

DO   "Number one was definitely hard. What are some good examples you could have used to demonstrate the concept?"

"For number three, most of you knew that X was wrong, but you couldn't explain why. What thoughts do you have about it now?"

"For number five, many of you got the gist of the essay, but you were short on specifics. What important points belong in this essay?"

"For number seven, you had the facts for the essay but trouble organizing. Let's get those facts up on the board and figure out how to get them in an order that makes sense."

Make the review instructive, not humiliating.

> DON'T   Call on specific students for answers and force them to reveal their shortcomings to their classmates.
>
> DO   Let students volunteer to answer questions with which they are comfortable or to contribute to an ongoing discussion of the correct answers.

Help students get the information they may be reluctant to request.

> DON'T   Make students ask about questions that they got wrong.
>
> DO   Emphasize that certain questions were hard for everyone and initiate the discussion of these questions yourself. And always invite your students to ask about questions you have not addressed if time is still available.

Late Work

Most teaching assistants penalize students for turning work in late. If you have a strict due date, it is only fair to the students who turn in their work on time to take points off for late assignments. You should decide at the beginning of the semester how you will deal with late assignments and make your policy clear in your syllabus. For example, many teaching assistants subtract part of a grade for every day that an assignment is overdue. By outlining your policy in advance and sticking to it, you (and your students) will not need to worry about whether you are being unfair by penalizing students for late work. When you grade an assignment that has been handed in late, be clear in your feedback about how the grade was influenced by lateness as opposed to the quality of the work (e.g., "B → B− (late)").

Think carefully before adopting a "no late work accepted" policy. Imagine a scenario in which a good, conscientious student misses a deadline by an hour because the power went out and their final grade suddenly drops by a full letter because you must give them a zero for the assignment.

▥ Missed Exams

The policy on missed exams may be dictated and announced by the professor of the course. If not, tell students in advance what will happen if they miss an exam. Given that students know the dates of the exams well in advance, it is not unreasonable to tell students that they should only miss an exam for illness or an emergency and that they should have proof of the reason for the absence. You can tell students that they will be allowed to make up an exam only if they bring you a note from a doctor or some proof of an emergency. If you are clear from the beginning of the semester that you have a strict policy about missed exams, you will be less likely to have students missing exams during the semester.

There are a few ways for a student to make up an exam.

- Write another exam that is sufficiently distinct from the one given in class and administer it to the student.
- Ask the student to write one or two short essays on topics that were covered by the exam.
- Consider the exam "missed" and double the weight of the following exam in the final grade.

What you do will depend on the nature and content of your course. What matters most is that you make your policy clear from the outset and that your policy does not unduly penalize students with a legitimate reason for missing the exam.

▥ Calculating Final Grades

This often tedious process can be dramatically accelerated by using a computer program with mathematical capabilities. It can track scores throughout the semester, and it can quickly and accurately compute final grades once the last assignments are entered.

Calculating Class Participation

Regardless of how objective you make your grading over the course of the semester, calculating class participation is inherently subjective. The best approach is to grade students relative to each other on this dimension. However, consider all of the ways students can participate in the class and take these into account when calculating a participation grade. For example, a student may have said very little in class but may have been an active contributor to a class email group. The grade should reflect the student's overall involvement in the course, not just their participation in group discussions. Calculating participation throughout the term can make the process easier and result in a more balanced assessment; two possible strategies are described here.

Grading Participation Weekly

One way to promote objectivity in grading participation is to make yourself grade each student's participation at the end of every week. This way, you can credit students for a particularly strong or weak performance that you may later forget. Then, at the end of the semester, you can average these weekly grades for an overall participation grade.

Having Students Grade Their Own Participation

In courses in which class participation is a critical part of the grade (e.g., foreign language classes), you may want to open a dialogue with students about their level of participation. On a regular basis (weekly or biweekly), you can ask students to submit a piece of paper on which they grade their own participation for that period and provide an explanation of the grade. You can return this paper during the next class meeting with your grade for them and an explanation of it. This way, students can be clear about your expectations and what they need to do to maintain or improve their participation grade.

Grading Final Exams and Papers

As you grade final work, particularly exams, bear in mind that for many courses, a significant number of students will not pick up the work once the course is over and they have received their grade. This does not mean that you should grade any less carefully, but you can limit your written comments. If you know that a student plans to pick up the work or has asked you to send it to their home, you can focus your efforts accordingly.

Returning Final Exams and Papers

Before the term ends, tell students how they can pick up or receive their final work. There are a few options.

- If appropriate, leave exams and papers with the support staff in your departmental office. Tell students that they can pick up their work during regular business hours.

- Schedule an extra set of office hours at the end of the grading period so that students can stop by to pick up their work.

- Tell students to turn in a stamped, self-addressed envelope with the exam or the final paper and you will mail the work to them.

We do not encourage you to leave a box of final work in the hall outside your office. This violates students' privacy and invites theft and destruction of property. Some universities even prohibit leaving student work in public areas like this. It is more difficult to schedule times and ways for students to pick up their work from you individually, but it is an important end to your contract with the students in the course.

Posting Final Grades

Final grades are now often available to students online within hours, if not minutes, after you submit them. Students may contact you with questions about the calculation of their final grade. Even though the term is technically over, it is your responsibility to address their questions, either in person or via email.

▣ Further Reading

Davis, B. G. 2009. *Tools for Teaching*. 2d. ed. San Francisco: Jossey-Bass.

Lowman, J. 1995. *Mastering the Techniques of Teaching*. 2d ed. San Francisco: Jossey-Bass.

Rotenberg, R. 2010. *The Art and Craft of College Teaching: A Guide for New Professors and Graduate Students*. 2d ed. Walnut Creek, CA: Left Coast Press.

Stevens, D. D., and A. J. Levi. 2005. *Introduction to Rubrics: An Assessment Tool to Save Time, Convey Effective Feedback, and Promote Student Learning*. Sterling, VA: Stylus.

Svinicki, M., and W. J. McKeachie. 2011. *McKeachie's Teaching Tips: Strategies, Research, and Theory for College and University Teachers*. 13th ed. Belmont, CA: Wadsworth.

Walvoord, B. E., and V. J. Anderson. 2010. *Effective Grading: A Tool for Learning and Assessment*. 2d ed. San Francisco: Jossey-Bass.

Zak, F., and C. C. Watson, eds. 1998. *The Theory and Practice of Grading Writing: Problems and Possibilities*. Albany: State University of New York Press.

8

One-on-One Interaction with Students

Managing a classroom of many students is a complex task; equally important and challenging is working with individual students both inside and outside the classroom. This chapter offers suggestions to make your one-on-one dealings with students as effective, efficient, and comfortable as possible.

◾ Office Hours

Most teaching assistants will hold one to three sets of office hours each week. This time is usually provided so that students can drop in for individualized information, clarification, or advice.

Where to Hold Office Hours

Graduate programs typically provide office space to teaching assistants. Even when such an office is available, some teaching assistants prefer to meet with students in a public place, such as a coffee shop or a student lounge. We strongly recommend using a departmental office for office hours; the potential problems with meeting in a public place outweigh the potential benefits. Never meet at your home. Here are some of the pros and cons of each setting.

Meeting in a Departmental Office

Pros It maintains your authority as a teacher and as a representative of the department for which you work.

It provides greater clarity about the nature of your meeting and your relationship with your students (specifically, that you are the teacher).

It helps maintain appropriate boundaries between students and teachers; it is the blurring of these boundaries that encourages both students and teachers to think of each other as potential romantic objects. To this end, always keep the door to your office open; for discussions of a grade or other sensitive issues, you may want to close the door partway and lower your voice.

Meeting in the privacy of an office is a courtesy to students who come to your office hours to discuss sensitive issues such as their grades or personal problems that are affecting their work in the course.

Cons It can set up a more formal relationship than some teaching assistants would like to have with their students. However, the tone of your relationship with your students depends more on your approach and attitude than on the location of your meeting.

Departmental offices often lack "ambiance."

Meeting in a Coffee Shop

Pros Many graduate students do not like their offices (typically windowless and "shoe-box" sized). And if no students come to office hours, it can be more pleasant to spend two hours in a coffee shop than in a shoe box.

It may make students feel that you are more accessible to them than university professors can sometimes seem to students.

CONS It can blur boundaries and lead to misunderstandings about the nature of your relationship with your students.

Students may feel obligated to purchase something, which may be a hardship.

Students may have trouble finding you in a crowded coffee shop, or they may not have a suitable place to wait if you are already meeting with another student (or graduate student friend) when they get there.

There can be many distractions in coffee shops.

It is easy for other patrons to eavesdrop on your meeting, which is not fair to students who come to discuss sensitive issues such as their grades.

If your department does not provide you an office, try to find a public space on campus where students can easily find you and your conversations are not likely to be overheard (e.g., a public room in a library or student union).

Timing Office Hours

You will save yourself and your students a lot of trouble by holding office hours at times when the students probably will attend. In other words, while you may be able to get a lot of your own work done if you hold your office hours from 7:00 to 9:00 AM, you will likely have to find other times during the week to meet with interested students. You may also want to consider making sure that your office hours are not at the same time each day. For example, if you hold office hours from 1:00 to 2:00 PM on Tuesdays and Thursdays, students who cannot come to the Tuesday time because of a class are likely to have the same class on Thursday. That said, also schedule your office hours such that they work well with your schedule and do not interrupt a long stretch of potential work time.

Naturally, you should be on time for your office hours and have all of the necessary course materials on hand. If you need to change your office hours, even for a week, notify your students in advance. If a student cannot attend your scheduled office hours, find another time when you both can meet.

Coordinating Student Meetings

How long you spend talking with one particular student will depend on the nature of the visit and how many other students are waiting to meet with you. If another student peers into your meeting, ask them to wait outside your office and tell them approximately how long the wait will be. After that period of time, tell the student in your office that to be fair, you need to meet with the student waiting outside the office.

Students Who Misuse Your Office Hours

You will occasionally come across students who are much better at making it to your office hours than they are at making it to your class. If a student starts coming to your office hours regularly to find out about what is going on in the section or the lecture (or both!), you will want to nip this behavior in the bud. The best approach is to inform the student kindly that you would be delighted to discuss and clarify any questions the student has about the section, lecture, or readings after the student has obtained class notes and reviewed all the material.

EXAMPLES "Do you know anyone else in the class from whom you could get notes? Then if you have questions, we could talk about those specifically."

"Have you done the required reading for this week? Much of the material we talked about in class is covered there, so let's talk about what seemed unclear to you in the reading."

This is also a good time to remind the student about your attendance policy and the potential effect of multiple absences on grades.

Ending Office Hours

If you are still meeting with a student when office hours end, feel free to state politely that your office hours are over. If necessary, offer to have the student return to your office hours next week to continue your discussion. Ending office hours can be difficult if you are in the middle of meeting with a student who is very upset or angry. Again, politely observe that your office hours have ended and that you can continue to talk with the student more in the future if necessary.

See pages 160–67 in this chapter, Students with Personal Problems, and pages 184–91 in this chapter, Grade Complaints, for more information on how to end office hours.

▣ Email

Answer all emails from your students within a reasonable time-frame, and you should send time-sensitive emails to students only if you know they check their mailboxes regularly. If a student seems to be emailing you excessively, suggest that the student come to your office hours so that you can answer a number of their questions at one time. A barrage of emails from a particular student can be the surface manifestation of a bigger issue (e.g., a student crush, excessive academic insecurity). Save all these email messages and monitor the situation so that you can manage further developments, if they arise. Refer to page 153, Students Who Misuse Your Office Hours, for information on how to address students who regularly email you for information instead of coming to class.

Email Tone

You can set the tone when you use email to communicate with your students. Some teaching assistants like to keep their emails formal, while other teaching assistants like to use email as a forum for more casual course-related discussion. If you feel that a student's emails are overly familiar, all you have to do is raise the level of formality of your response; most students will get the hint.

From a student:

Dear Sam,

I am in your Math 250 class. I was not in class on Wed. Sept 20th, due to the fact that I was suffering from a migraine headache. I was wondering if I could turn in my assignment for that day on Friday. If so I would really appreciate it. I do not have a doctor's note, but I do have prescribed medication that I can show you if it is necessary. My migraines bring me to the point of near stroke, thereby rendering me unfit to attend class. I will describe it in further detail if need be. Please write and let me know if I can turn in my assignment. I understand your attendance policy and will accept a negative answer if you must give one. I look forward to hearing from you.

Your student, Peter

Your formal response:

Peter,

Thank you for the note explaining your absence. I will accept the assignment on Friday and will not mark it down, although the absence will have to count as one of the three absences you are allowed during the term. I hope you are feeling better, and I'll see you on Friday.

Sam

Your informal response:

Hi Peter. Thanks for the note. Your migraines sound miserable! I hope you are feeling recovered by this time—I hate to think of you teetering on the edge of stroke-dom. :-) Yes, I will accept your assignment on Friday, and I will give you full credit, given the nature of your absence. But I'm afraid that we'll have to count it as one of your three absences. Take care of that head, and I'll see you on Friday. —Sam

Email and CCing

If an email conversation with a student becomes antagonistic or sensitive or if you are discussing matters that may require departmental intervention, CC (i.e., send a copy to) the professor and/or the director of undergraduate studies in your response (and include the student's original message). This way, the professor or director of undergraduate studies can monitor the situation and understand the details of the interaction if you later need advice or intervention. It also automatically brings in a third party to defuse the personal nature of the interaction between you and your student. The presence of a "higher authority" may or may not alter the student's behavior, but it reminds them that your relationship is part of an institutional hierarchy.

Email Records

Save all of your emails from each of the courses that you teach for the duration of the semester (at least). This will provide you with an easily accessible record of your communications with students. Create a class file and save all class-related email there, both messages from students and your responses (if you CC yourself in your response, you will be more likely to remember to save it).

Students with Attendance Problems

Some college students feel they should not have to abide by attendance or lateness policies. If you have a formal attendance policy, spell out explicitly on the syllabus how many absences students are allowed and how students' grades will be affected by additional absences. Also tell students the point in time (e.g., 20 minutes) at which "lateness" becomes an absence (otherwise students may come to the last ten minutes of class to avoid an absence). Then, be consistent in enforcing the policy or some students may exploit your leniency.

Handling Student Excuses

Once students have used their allowed number of absences, they often will come to you with a distressing or complicated story about their next absence. Their story may well be true, but that does not necessarily make it an excused absence. Sympathize with their predicament, but firmly explain that if it were not for their previous absences, this absence would not be a problem. Allowed absences are not meant as days when students can skip class; you provide them knowing that emergencies can arise during the semester and students may have to miss class. If your students do not need them, they should not use these allowed absences.

Handling Excessive Student Absence

Students will usually miss multiple classes for two reasons: (1) they don't care about the class, or (2) something has gone very wrong in their personal lives. The first case is often grounds for failure, especially if students also are not handing in work. Do not feel guilty about this—these students know they deserve to fail for such behavior.

Students who miss many classes for personal reasons, unfortunately, still may have missed too many classes to do well or perhaps even to pass the course. If they won't be able to attend all future classes and make up missed work, you can offer to give them a withdrawal from the class or an incomplete rather than failing them. It is your responsibility as an instructor not to pass students who do not complete the work in the course for whatever reason, but you usually have the option to authorize the student's withdrawal from the course rather than fail them. Again, you will want to diagnose this problem before deciding on a solution.

> See pages 160–67 in this chapter, Students with Personal Problems, for more information.

▣ Students with Learning Disabilities

The Nature of Learning Disabilities

Universities and their students are increasingly aware that there are competent students who also have learning disabilities. There is no relationship between being intelligent and having a learning disability; students with learning disabilities simply have some specific difficulty receiving or communicating information in one or more of the ways that are most common in academic settings.

What the Student Should Do

It is up to the student to alert you to their learning disability and tell you what kind of special accommodations they need before the first assignments are due or the first exam is administered. Students should come to you at the beginning of the term with official documentation of the problem and a request for special assistance. Any student with a learning disability should be able to provide a letter from the appropriate university office. This documentation likely will specify what you should do as an instructor and ensure that privileges associated with learning disabilities are not abused.

What the Teaching Assistant Should Do

Put a note on your syllabus asking students with learning disabilities or other special needs that you will need to accommodate to notify you immediately. When a student comes to you about a learning disability, you should make every effort to accommodate their special needs. However, you are not under any obligation to provide retroactive help to a student who alerts you to their learning disability after they already have had trouble in your class. Ask them what special accommodations they need for the next assignment or exam, and encourage them to tell their other instructors about the learning disability as soon as possible.

If you feel that a student's requests for special accommodations are unreasonable, contact the university office that issued the official documentation for advice on what is considered appropriate.

Student: I want to talk to you about my grade on the last exam. I didn't do very well, and part of the problem is that I have a learning disability that makes it hard for me to work under time pressure.

TA: I am glad you let me know that you have a learning disability that got in the way of your performance on the exam. If this is causing you such serious problems, you should get documentation from the student services office that specifies the kinds of accommodations you need. Then we can arrange what you need for the next exam. In the future, you should let your instructors know about your disability at the beginning of the semester so that you get the support you need for the whole semester.

Student: Well, it works for me to take the same exam as everyone else but to just have more time to do it. But I am also worried that this bad first exam will hurt my grade in the course.

TA: Okay, if you can get me the documentation of the learning disability, it should be no problem to arrange for you to get extra time. As for the last exam, it would not be fair to the other students to let you retake the exam, even with your disability. This is why it is important that you let your instructors know about your disability at the beginning of the semester rather than waiting until you get a disappointing grade.

Students with Personal Problems

The Nature of Personal Problems

There are students with personal problems, and these problems often affect their academic performance. College students are at least as likely to suffer from troubles such as depression, eating disorders, drug or alcohol abuse, and violent relationships as are people in the "real world." You may become aware of a student's personal problems in a number of ways. Sometimes, a student will identify you as a caring person in a position of authority and will come to you directly, send you an email, or attach a note to an assignment to alert you to the problem. Other times, you will become aware of a student's personal problem when it interferes with the student's ability to do their work in your course.

What the Teaching Assistant Should Do

It is not your job to diagnose or treat the problem. While you will want to be supportive of your students, you will compromise your role as a teacher if you also try to be a therapist. Do not try to solve the student's problem. What you *can* do is help the student become aware of how their problem is interfering with their performance in your class (if they are not already aware of it) and point them toward help. Many university campuses offer free mental health services and academic counseling to students. It is highly likely that at some point you will come across a student who needs some sort of counseling; make a point of finding out about what services are available at your university.

It is a very natural reaction to want to accommodate the student as much as possible, especially if they seem upset, penitent, or frantic. But you may not be doing them a favor if you excuse them from the responsibilities of the class. If their problem is such that they cannot handle their academic workload, they must confront this situation and seek outside help. They may need counseling or time off from school. Think of it as a "strict parent policy" in which you are enforcing fair rules and teaching students how to fulfill their responsibilities. Additionally, you can express your understanding that there are some semesters when difficult life events take priority over schoolwork. What is critical is that the student meet the problem head-on so that they can prioritize school again as soon as possible.

Recognizing Students with Personal Problems

A student's personal problems often will be quite severe before they significantly affect academic performance. You should not approach a student about a personal problem unless you are quite sure that something is going wrong for that student outside of the classroom. While you may be able to speculate about what is going wrong, you will have the most effective conversation with a student if you focus on what you do know: how the student is doing in your class. For example, you may notice that a student misses class often and smells of alcohol when they do come. Or a student may seem to be extremely "down" and ask for repeated extensions on papers because they are unable to work productively.

Reaching Out to Students with Personal Problems

If you need to talk with a student about the ways a personal problem is affecting their work in the class, be sure to do it at a time and place where the student is likely to feel comfortable and where the conversation will not be overheard. Your departmental office may be a good place for a meeting like this. If you do not have a planned conference with the student, you will need to make a time to meet with them. If you need to plan a meeting, ask the student to stay after class and then make sure that you get them to set up a meeting with you.

TA: Jamie, I want to talk with you about your work for the class. Could you meet with me on Wednesday at 4:00?

Student: No, I have practice then.

TA: O.K., when are some times next week that would work for you to meet?

What to Say in the Meeting

Regardless of what is going wrong for the student, once you have arranged a meeting, you can talk with your student about their work and suggest extra help in the following manner.

> EXAMPLE "Jamie, I've noticed that you are missing class a lot lately and that you failed the most recent exam after getting a B+ on the first one. It seems like things outside of class may be making it hard for you to do your best in here. If you are interested, there are support services around campus, such as the counseling center, which can help you relieve stresses that are getting in the way of your academic work. I wanted to talk with you to find ways for you to do the best work you can in the course right now."

Keep your focus on the student's performance in the class. You and the student must determine if and how they can improve their performance in the class and how you can assist in *that* process.

When a Student "Blows You Off"

It is the student's prerogative not to take your advice. In this case, be sure that you are clear with the student about where they stand academically and then do not pursue the issue further. Do not consider your efforts wasted: some people will seek out much-needed counseling only after they have heard the suggestion from a variety of people.

When a Student Approaches You

More commonly, a student will come to you to discuss a personal problem. When this happens, be sensitive to what they are telling you, without letting them "spill" too much. If you allow a student to give you an overly detailed account of their personal problem (e.g., confusion about how to handle their girlfriend's pregnancy), you risk blurring the boundary between being their teacher and being their friend or counselor. As soon as feels comfortable, you can use these guidelines to respond to the student:

- Acknowledge the problem and be sympathetic.

  EXAMPLE   "You were right to let me know that this has
  been going on for you, and it sounds really
  stressful. It is not uncommon for people to
  have trouble with (depression/eating disor-
  ders/romantic or family relationships)."

- If it feels like an appropriate time, tell the student about
  the university services available to help them with their
  problem.

  EXAMPLE   "Sometimes, it can really help to talk with
  someone about this kind of problem. If you
  are feeling like it would help to talk to someone besides your family and friends, you
  could contact the university counseling center,
  which has services available to students for
  just this sort of situation."

- Talk with the student about where they stand in your class
  and how you can work together to get them caught up on
  the work. If the student's mood makes it impossible to
  have a productive conversation, arrange for a future meeting.

When a Student Has Diagnosed Mental Health Problems

In the last several years, the number of college students with psychiatric diagnoses (such as attention deficit disorder, major depres-
sive disorder, generalized anxiety disorder, and bipolar disorder)
has increased dramatically. Over a recent 13-year time frame, college counseling centers reported that the number of students presenting with anxiety, depression, or suicidality doubled. Further,
the number of college students taking prescription psychiatric
medication increased from 10 to 25 percent during this same
period. While it is impossible to know exactly what factors account
for the increased number of college students with psychiatric diagnoses, teaching assistants today are often confronted with students

who struggle in class due to a psychiatric diagnosis for which the student is already receiving medication, psychotherapy, or both.

As with personal problems, teaching assistants often become aware of a student's mental health diagnosis when the student is having difficulty meeting the demands of the course. Though a student may come to you asking for accommodations due to their diagnosis, you should not feel obliged to provide such accommodations. This is true even when a student brings a note from a clinician informing you of the student's diagnostic and treatment status and requesting accommodations. For chronic or ongoing conditions (including mental health issues), all requests for accommodation should come from the university's office for students with disabilities—typically learning and physical disabilities. This way, instructors are not put in the position of having to make student-by-student decisions about whether and which accommodations should be granted.

- If a student's mental health status poses a concern early in the semester, talk with the student about whether your course is an appropriate choice at that time.

  EXAMPLE   "Thank you for letting me know about your diagnosis and its impact on your work for our class. I am glad to support you over the course of the semester, but will be unable to modify the course for you without documentation from the university office for students with disabilities. If you suspect that you will need accommodations to manage this course, let's think about whether this is the best course for you, or the best time for you to take this course."

- If a student's mental health status becomes a concern once the semester is well underway, talk with the student about whether they will be able to continue in your course.

EXAMPLE   "Thank you for letting me know about your
            diagnosis and its impact on your work for our
            class. If you have documentation from the uni-
            versity office for students with disabilities, I
            can grant you the accommodations specified
            in the documentation, but I'm unable to grant
            accommodations retroactively. As always, I am
            here to support your efforts to complete the
            course. However, if you feel that you may not
            be able to complete this course in a way you
            feel good about, withdrawing from the course
            may make more sense than continuing."

After talking with a student about the impact of their mental
health diagnosis on their progress in your course, consider documenting your conversation in a follow-up email to the student. In
your email, you can again express your support for the student, the
ways in which you can be of help, and remind the student of the
other resources on campus that might be of use.

EXAMPLE   Dear Jean,

            I'm glad we had a chance to talk in office
            hours today about the challenges you are fac-
            ing this semester. Please know that I am glad
            to work with you in office hours, or in addi-
            tional appointments as needed, to support
            your efforts in our class. As I mentioned in our
            meeting, the office for students with disabili-
            ties may be able to help you secure further
            support this semester or in the semesters to
            come. Do let me know if I can help you get in
            touch with them.

            Sincerely,

            Tom

When a Student Mentions Suicide

Sometimes students will refer either directly or indirectly to thoughts of suicide. You as an instructor must treat these comments with the utmost seriousness. You will need to notify the counseling services at your school about the student's comments.

If a student mentions suicide to you in a conversation, you may feel at a loss for a response. You can start by trying to assess the immediacy of the threat by asking whether they are expressing the intensity of their distress at that moment or are talking about a wish they might consider acting on. If the student indicates that there is any possibility they might act on suicidal impulses, let them know that you will need to act on what they have told you. Call counseling services immediately and ask about how to proceed. You may end up walking with the student to counseling services.

> EXAMPLE   "That you are letting me know that you are thinking about hurting yourself tells me that you are looking for help. It's my job to get you to the right help. Let's call counseling services right now."

Even if the student protests that they don't want you to tell anyone, you must call counseling services. You can tell the student that you are doing your job—it is required of you to do this.

If the student says that they have no intention of harming themselves, acknowledge to them that they seem very distressed and ask if they are getting help. Depending on the nature of the student's response, you may call counseling services with the student still in your office or you may call them later to report the interaction. In any event, if a student mentions suicide, you need to call counseling services to let them know what has occurred.

When a Student Cannot Do the Work

Sometimes a student's problems will become so overwhelming that they stop attending class or cannot do the required work. You must step in at this point and alert the student that they cannot pass the course given this situation. If you feel the student's problems justify it, you can offer to withdraw them from the course rather than failing them. Do not feel guilty about this kind of action. These students know that they are incapable of doing the work, and they are rarely surprised by such consequences. While you may feel tempted to bend over backward to help the student through your class, this behavior may not be as helpful as you think it is. Many people will get adequate help for severe personal problems only when they are faced with a clear consequence related to the problem, such as having to withdraw from a class. Be firm but also remember that it is important to express sympathy within appropriate boundaries; authority figures who are not appropriately sympathetic can be very hurtful.

Students Displaying Frightening or Bizarre Behavior

Sadly, the last several years have been marked by deadly shootings on university campuses. In the wake of these incidents, most universities have developed teams of faculty and staff to address concerns about students that engage in frightening, threatening, or bizarre behavior. You may become aware of alarming behavior through a student's comments in class or office hours, a student's email messages, or a student's written work.

If you have a student whose behavior concerns you, err on the side of caution. Report the student's behavior to the faculty member for your course and/or the chair of your department so that you can decide together on next steps. It may be necessary to alert a unit at the university responsible for addressing concerning student behavior and/or intervening when required. In less extreme circumstances, you will want to talk through with the faculty member strategies for approaching the student about their concerning behavior. While some of this student behavior can seem bizarre or scary, sometimes these students are in real personal distress and need help; they may well appreciate your genuine concern for their well-being.

As soon as you become aware of this kind of situation, keep copies of all communication with the student and all student work. Send emails to yourself or your professor/supervisor documenting interactions in office hours or class. This kind of record can become very important.

Antagonistic Students

You will have antagonistic students. At times, students will make comments or write papers that are more antagonistic than thoughtful. Though some students will do this by design, others will not even be aware they are being offensive or antagonistic. Your first reaction may be to protect yourself or other students from potential harm caused by an antagonistic student's words. But your role as a teacher allows you to deal with these circumstances in a way that is constructive, not simply defensive. You want to promote intellectual disagreement; it is critical to a serious and productive learning environment. It is your job to help students present arguments and counterarguments that can be taken seriously.

See page 62 in Chapter 4, The Antagonistic Debater, for more information on how to handle this behavior in class.

Problematic Terminology

Sometimes students will unknowingly use terms or phrases that are offensive to you or to their fellow students. Sometimes students will knowingly use offensive terminology in order to antagonize you or their fellow students. First you'll need to make a diagnosis: is the offense intentional or not?

If the student is using offensive language unwittingly, it usually only takes one comment (spoken or written) to remedy this situation. Gently explain to the student that there are more accepted terms and that they should be aware of the connotations of the terms they are presently using.

If the student is being deliberately offensive, you still need to see this as a teachable moment, both for the student and for their classmates. It is your responsibility to ensure that your classroom is a comfortable and productive learning environment. You can take this opportunity to talk with students about the wider ramifications of this kind of language and its power to derail any discourse, including a classroom discussion. Assuming that the student has a valid point to make, you can also show the student how this phrasing serves only to undermine the effectiveness of their argument.

> See page 63 in Chapter 4, The Bomb Dropper, for more information on how to handle this behavior in class.

Problematic Arguments

At times, students will mistake polemic for proof. This is especially likely when students have strong personal and antagonistic feelings about an issue. Your best approach is to show students how weak a proofless polemic is. Push students (either in spoken discussion or in written comments) to defend their positions with specific facts and a recognition of the merits of their argument in light of

"I had a first-year student who used the word *queer* to refer to things he thought were weird. I pulled him aside two weeks into class and gently explained to him how and why that word might be offensive to his classmates. He was shocked: the term was used at his high school all the time, and he had no idea it could be offensive."

opposing views. Antagonistic arguments are often based on generalizations and empty rhetoric. When grading papers with these kinds of arguments you can show students (with your comments and their grade) that this kind of argument—antagonistic or not—is not effective. If your grading is based on the quality of the argument, you can explain it to the student without having to engage in a personal discussion of your views on this particular issue.

When Reason Fails

In extreme cases, you may find that talking with an antagonistic student or writing reasonable comments on their papers is failing to curb their behavior. You can begin by consulting with the professor or with the director of undergraduate studies about how to control the student's behavior in class or how to respond effectively to their written assignments. Make and keep copies of the student's antagonistic writing if you feel that you may need to seek advice from other teachers. If any part of your inter-action with this student is occur-ring on email, CC (i.e., send a copy to) the professor and/or the director of undergraduate studies to keep them informed on how the situation is progressing. The director of undergraduate studies has the authority and responsi-bility to meet with students if their behavior becomes disrup-tive and to transfer them to another section if necessary.

These situations can prove to be personally upsetting. Use the professor and your col-leagues as moral support so that you are not drawn into a per-sonal debate with the student. You will never gain by letting yourself become visibly angry or irrational with the student, so find other outlets for your frus-tration, hurt, or anger.

"Once I had a student who wrote a paper entitled 'Democrats Suck.' He had clearly written it to antagonize me, to see what I would do. I gave him a D. I gave him that grade not because I disagreed with him but because the paper was terribly writ-ten. He immediately emailed me to ask for a conference about the grade. I knew it was going to be an unpleasant confer-ence, and beforehand, I went over all the problems in the argument and in the proof so that I felt prepared. When I met with him, I was open about our differ-ences in political views, and I acknowl-edged that some of his criticisms of liberals were potentially strong points. I then pointed out all the structural weak-nesses in the paper itself. I pushed him for specifics to back up his generaliza-tions and pointed out his leaps in logic. He walked away angry, but more with writing than with me."

Fraternizing with Students

Social Activities with Students

Though you may like many of your students, it is not appropriate to include them in your social circle while you are their instructor. Socializing with your students can compromise your professional authority. Students are not necessarily prepared to think of you both as a peer and as an authority figure; it is critical that you not compromise the latter in an effort to "connect" with your students. In addition, socializing with your students exposes you to all sorts of risks.

- Many students drink illegally; you do not want to be a part of this activity, even as a witness.
- Spending time with your students as a peer encourages them to think of you as a potential romantic interest.
- Spending time with your students as a peer encourages them to think they can ask you favors about grades, exams, or other course work as a friend.
- Here is a scenario to avoid: a student blithely mentions to their parents that they were out drinking with their teaching assistant on Friday night. The parents call your department to ask about the appropriateness of that behavior.

You have lots of people who can be your friends. Let your students be your students. So, if you are invited to come to a student party or to join your students for a drink after class, thank them for the invitation and tell them that you cannot make it.

Socializing with former students, once the term is over, can still be problematic. They or their friends may take classes from you in the future, and appropriate teacher-student boundaries may be more difficult to maintain. However, one potentially rewarding part of teaching is maintaining ongoing mentoring relationships with some students. Use your judgment in establishing such relationships.

Crushes

Crushes can go both ways. However, it is more common for students to develop crushes on their teaching assistants. These crushes often are harmless, as both the student and the instructor know that the student has no plans to pursue this romantic possibility. Ignore these crushes unless the student decides to act on their feelings. Be firm in turning down invitations for social activities and, if necessary, tell the student explicitly that romantic relationships between students and instructors are not appropriate.

> *Student:* I was wondering if you would want to grab coffee with me sometime.
>
> *TA:* If you would like to talk about the course, I would be happy to talk with you during my office hours or to make another appointment if that time doesn't work.
>
> *Student:* No, I was just wanting to grab coffee and hang out.
>
> *TA:* I appreciate the offer, but I find that it doesn't work for teaching assistants and students to hang out together socially.
>
> *Student:* Right, but I was thinking that we could just get to know each other better.
>
> *TA:* Well, thank you for asking, but like I said, it won't work.
>
> *Student:* Well, how about when the semester's over?
>
> *TA:* I really don't think that will be feasible.

Teaching assistants also can find particular students attractive. Do not act on this attraction and be careful not to show any favoritism toward a student you find attractive. Do not allow yourself to consider the possibility of a romantic relationship with a student, even as something to be discussed as a "future possibility." Do not dabble in the gray areas (e.g., inviting a student "just" for coffee); most students will feel obliged to accept such an invitation even if they would rather not—a situation that could feel to a student like sexual harassment.

Once the term is over, you are technically free to do as you please at most schools, taking into account that your responsibilities as an instructor can extend beyond the term (requests for recommendations, enrollment in another course with you). But during the term, you should in no way jeopardize your teacher-student relationship.

Attraction between students and teaching assistants is a tricky area. You must not forget that the power dynamic of the classroom affects *all* of your relationships with students, including ones that feel like genuine attraction. The difference between romance and sexual harassment is that sexual harassment involves a power differential that could potentially be abused.

> **"The second time I taught first-year composition, I had 16 first-year men in the class, about ten of whom stared at me with adoring, puppy-dog eyes during every class meeting. And they would come to my office hours all the time. 'I have an idea for my paper—can I come talk to you about it?' 'Will you take a look at my rough draft?' 'Will you read my new introduction?' But it was all very safe (and very endearing). I knew they weren't going to do anything about these crushes, and they knew they weren't going to do anything either. And, whatever their motives, their writing sure did get a lot better!"**

Sexual Harassment

Sexual harassment involves an abuse of power. Teachers always have more institutional power than students; students sometimes have more physical or cultural power than teachers. Sexual harassment between teachers and students can go both ways. Instructors may be sexually harassed by a student, but it usually happens the other way around.

Sexual Harassment by Teaching Assistants

You are in the position of authority with regard to your students; you must, therefore, be especially careful not to abuse your power. Many teaching assistants are close enough in age to their students that they may flirt with the idea of having a romantic encounter with one of them. These thoughts may be fueled by the fact that students often have crushes on their teaching assistants. Under no circumstances should you pursue a romantic and/or sexual relationship with a current student. In addition, you should never do *anything* that might be construed by a reasonable person as a sexual advance.

DON'T Touch your students.

Make suggestive comments to them.

Use "racy" or sexually explicit language inappropriately in class.

Ask students to read "racy" or explicit material aloud in class or to write sexually explicit or provocative papers.

Invite a student for a "datelike" encounter (e.g., coffee, lunch, a movie).

Encourage a student to call you at home.

Call a student at home unless absolutely necessary for class-related business; whenever possible, use e-mail.

Meet with a student at your home—or theirs—even about strictly academic matters.

Meet with a student behind closed doors. If a student has come to you about a personal problem, lowered voices can provide the necessary privacy. See pages 160–67, Students with Personal Problems, in this chapter for more information on how to handle this situation.

Discuss your personal life with your students.

These guidelines hold for students of the opposite sex or of the same sex. It is a mistake to think that sexual harassment occurs only across sexes.

While these guidelines are designed to protect your students, they also protect you. At the most basic level, you do not want to do anything that would expose you to an accusation of sexual harassment. More generally, you do not want to compromise your position as an educator or your students' ability to feel comfortable learning in your classroom.

Sexual Harassment by Students

Defining Sexual Harassment by Students

The standards for what constitutes sexual harassment by a student are slightly different than those for harassment by an instructor. Without the power differential to abuse, harassment in this case is defined as any action that continues after an explicit "no." Anything that feels like sexual harassment needs to be stopped as quickly as possible. Sexual harassment by a student can include (but is not limited to) these examples.

EXAMPLES A student makes subtle sexual comments to you after you have told them this is inappropriate.

A student asks you out for a date again after you definitively have said "no" the first time.

A student says grossly inappropriate things to you after you have told them what they are doing is inappropriate.

A student tries to touch you in a sexual way.

Responding to Sexual Harassment by Students

Your response needs to be firm and authoritative. If any part of this kind of interaction occurs on email, send a copy of your responses to the director of undergraduate studies (including the student's original message) to defuse the personal nature of the conversation and to alert the director to a potentially problematic situation.

EXAMPLES If the student says things to you that make you uncomfortable, you may tell the student that their comments are inappropriate and leave it at that. If the student continues this behavior, you can tell them that you will be forced to report them because this kind of behavior constitutes harassment.

If you are asked on a date, you can say that it is not appropriate for teaching assistants to date their students. Saying, "I'm sorry, I'm busy" is not a definitive "no."

If the student makes grossly inappropriate comments after you have told them to stop or tries to touch you in a sexual way, you have a choice to make: you can report the behavior to the proper campus authorities immediately, or you can tell the student that their behavior is not acceptable and that you will report it to the campus authorities if it happens again.

These situations are uncomfortable and unpleasant. Do not let your discomfort prevent you from responding with clarity and authority.

Most universities have an office that handles issues of sexual harassment. You should feel free to consult this office, the professor for the course, or the director of undergraduate studies for advice and moral support, even if you are uncertain about whether you will file a formal complaint.

▣ Plagiarism

Find out about your university's policy on plagiarism and explain this to students (in all seriousness) early in the term. If students will write papers for the course, carefully review how outside information (quotations and ideas) must be cited. Leave no room for questions about what constitutes plagiarism or the repercussions for doing it. Explain to your students that they may have their own questions about the proper citation of sources and that they should feel free to look to you for answers.

Minimizing Opportunities for Plagiarism

The best way to avoid plagiarism is to design assignments so specific to your course that students will not be able to copy material. Alternatively, or in addition, ask to see drafts of an assignment or have students discuss preliminary ideas with you (it is very hard to plagiarize a rough draft).

In addition, tell your students that you know about the term papers that are available in most fraternities and sororities and that you are familiar with the term-paper websites (even if you aren't!). If students know that you are clued in to these resources, they will be less likely to risk using them.

Helping Students Use the Internet Appropriately

With the growing popularity of the Internet, many students will do a preliminary Internet search on a topic before embarking on a paper or project. The Internet can be a valuable research tool if students know how to use it as such; you should explain to students the scholarly value of different types of Internet sites in your field and how they can begin to identify and use them. The Internet is also challenging traditional notions of copyright and plagiarism. Review with students how to cite information found on the Internet, whether it be general ideas or specific quotations.

Spotting Plagiarism

There are often fairly clear signals of plagiarism.

- The topic of the paper is only marginally related to the assignment.
- The tone or style of the paper is noticeably different from the student's previous work.
- The paper contains statistics, references, or facts that are not readily accessible to the student.
- There are very few usage issues or even unclear sentences.
- Two students hand in papers that are strikingly similar in the presentation and sequence of ideas.

Students sometimes will intersperse their own sentences or paragraphs into the plagiarized text, and you will notice shifts in style, tone, and grammatical correctness among these sections.

Unfortunately, you must accept that you will miss a certain amount of plagiarism. There are term papers on file in most fraternities and sororities, and there are now websites of term papers on the Internet. Because these resources are widely available, you should tailor assignments to make most of these so-called "model papers" useless for your students.

EXAMPLES   Find a magazine advertisement that you think is interesting. Describe the techniques it employs to sell the product. Attach the advertisement to the paper when you hand it in.

Imagine that you are writing the introduction to a volume of articles that includes the articles by Sanchez and Miller that we have read. In 500 words, explain to readers how the articles' arguments intersect.

Checking for Plagiarism

If you suspect a paper has been plagiarized, you have a few relatively quick options to check to see whether you can find the true source.

- Do a Lexis/Nexis or ProQuest search on the topic to find any relevant news articles that the student might have used.
- Search academic indexes for relevant scholarly articles.
- Do an Internet search on the topic.
- Type a suspicious phrase or sentence (surrounded by quotation marks) into Google.

There is a good chance, however, that you will not be able to identify the source; do not waste much of your time in this pursuit.

> "One semester I caught two students turning in virtually the same paper. Plagiarism doesn't get much more obvious than that! I told both students that they would be failed for the paper and might be referred to the board for academic discipline. But when I told the professor what I had done, he said, 'Oh no, in a case like this, I simply ask the students to rewrite the papers.' So, I then had to go back to the students and report the professor's decision. Needless to say, I felt like my authority as their teacher was shot for the rest of the semester."

Meeting with the Professor

Before you talk with the student about the paper, you should alert the professor that there may be a problem and decide on a course of action. You can draw on the professor's experience with these matters. You also want to make sure that you and the professor agree on how the matter should be handled.

Using University Resources

Most colleges and universities have offices that handle academic misconduct by students. You should feel free to consult with them at any point in the process as you decide upon a course of action. You may also want or need to forward the case to that office, after talking with the student, for a final determination on the case and for any sanctions at the university level (e.g., academic probation). University administrators ask instructors to alert their office about a student's academic misconduct so that they can determine whether this is a one-time offense or part of a larger pattern.

Tempering Your Reaction

If you think or know that a student has plagiarized a paper, it is easy to feel angry and offended. But initially you must give the student the benefit of the doubt and allow them to explain if they can. Even if you have thoroughly discussed plagiarism in class, some students will not understand that, for example, rephrasing material from a source without citing it constitutes plagiarism. Or some students will quote parts of a text and copy other parts of the same text without realizing that their citations do not cover the unquoted material.

Therefore, see your first job as "investigating the nature of the crime" to determine the circumstances and intentions. Start by saying, "I was wondering where you got this information." The student may innocently tell you the source, and then you can discuss appropriate citation of secondary material. If the student claims the work is their own and you know it is not, then you have a clear case of plagiarism.

Talking with the Student

You should always talk with the student about a plagiarized or suspicious paper. The student should have the opportunity to explain what happened before any further action is taken. You can email the student before you return papers and say that you need to set up a meeting to talk about the paper. Or when you return papers, you can tell the student that you need to meet with them individually to talk about the paper before you can grade it.

A Clear Case of Plagiarism

If you have the source of a plagiarized paper, we encourage you not to play games with the student by asking them how they came up with the idea. You can simply show the student the source and their paper and say, "Please explain to me how this happened."

An Unclear Case of Plagiarism

If you strongly suspect plagiarism, start the conversation by telling the student that, after reading the paper, you realized that you need to speak with them before you could grade it. There are then several ways to proceed.

Ask the student to tell you more about a confusing or interesting idea in the paper; this will quickly reveal the student's grasp of the material.

- Ask the student why they chose to write on this topic—and feel free to push them hard for a reason.
- Point to a passage that does not sound like their writing and ask them about the shift in tone or style.
- Ask the student to talk more about a source they cite in the paper.

Your suspicions will quickly become clear to the student, and that is unavoidable. Sometimes it will also quickly become clear that the student cannot talk knowledgeably about the paper. In this case, stop the conversation and simply ask, "Explain to me why you cannot talk about your paper." Sometimes the student will be able to talk knowledgeably about the paper, in which case you may not have any solid grounds for suspecting plagiarism.

The Dynamics of the Conversation

When students are pushed and realize that they have been "found out," they will sometimes admit guilt and plead extenuating circumstances. Students may also beg you to handle the case "in house" rather than alerting the professor or university office. The student will often frame the situation as if you had a choice about how to proceed. You should remind the student that they have put you in a position in which you must alert particular administrators about their academic misconduct.

> EXAMPLE   "I appreciate your honesty, and I too am sorry
> that we're having to have this conversation. But
> plagiarism is serious and needs to be dealt with
> at the departmental and university level."

At the end of all conversations about plagiarism, you do not need to have the answer ready about what will happen next; often you will find that you need time to think about the situation and talk with the professor or director of undergraduate studies. You can tell the student that the conversation has helped you to understand more about the situation and that you will get back to them about what will happen next.

If the student becomes belligerent or offended and does not admit to any wrongdoing, yet you still believe that the student has not written all of the material in the paper, you should end the conversation. There is little to gain by arguing with the student; you will need to bring in a third party, whether that is the professor, the director of undergraduate studies, or a university administrator.

> EXAMPLE   "It seems that we see this situation differently.
> Let's stop for now so that I can consult with Pro-
> fessor Marshall, and I'll get back to you about
> what will happen next."

Follow-Up to the Conversation
After your conversation with the student, you (and the professor, if appropriate) will have a choice to make. You may decide to turn the matter over to the appropriate university office for a decision and possible action. You do not need to be certain about the suspected plagiarism case to do this; you only need to have a strong suspicion of wrongdoing. A student who is found to have committed academic misconduct by this office will likely face consequences at the university level (e.g., academic probation). You

must then work with the course professor to determine appropriate consequences for the student in your course (e.g., failing the paper, failing the course).

If the student's protests have left you with serious doubts about whether plagiarism occurred, you may decide to deal with the matter yourself. Again, talk with the professor teaching the course to decide how to proceed. For example, the student can be asked to redo the assignment, to do the same assignment with better citations, and so forth. In some cases, you will simply have to swallow your suspicions and grade the paper. At some point, it is no longer a good use of your time to try to track down sources of papers you suspect are plagiarized.

In both clear and suspected cases of plagiarism, keep copies of all the student's work in case you are faced with another suspected violation of academic codes of conduct by the same student later in the term.

Enforcing Plagiarism Policies

If the plagiarism is the result of honest ignorance (e.g., if the student rephrased sentences without citing the source as opposed to copying entire paragraphs or an entire paper), you can see your meeting with them as a warning and as an important part of the student's education. Admonish them about the seriousness of plagiarism and alert them to the fact that they probably will not see such leniency again in their academic career. Ask the student to rewrite the paper and then grade it.

If it is a case of blatant plagiarism and you have identified the source or the student has confessed, consult with the professor for the course or the director of undergraduate studies and then follow the university's policy for handling this offense. There are no extenuating circumstances that make plagiarism acceptable. Because plagiarism is arguably the gravest offense at a university, it is critical that you take it seriously. Allow the university board for academic discipline to handle the matter.

▣ Cheating

Cheating often is not hard to catch if you are alert and watch for it during an exam.

Proctoring Exams

There are easy steps to take to minimize the opportunities for cheating.

- Ask students to move their desks apart (if the desks are movable).
- Ask students to sit in every other seat in a lecture hall with fixed chairs.
- Make students put all papers, books, and cell phones into their bags and close them.
- Walk around the room during the exam period, and if you are sitting in the front, look up often.
- If any students are acting suspicious, watch them carefully (do not be subtle about this) or stand near them.
- Ask students wearing baseball caps to take them off or wear them bill backward so that you can see where their eyes are looking.
- Create two forms of the same exam—the forms can have the same questions but in a different order.

Catching Cheating

If you are proctoring an exam and catch a student using a "cheat sheet" (or a "cheat cap" or a "cheat arm"), *quietly* confiscate the illegal material (if possible!). Ask the student where they are in the exam and mark that spot. Say to the student, "Finish the exam. I will discuss this with you when I grade the exams." If it is not possible to confiscate the material (without the amputation of a limb), take the student's exam and ask them to sit quietly until everyone else is finished in order to avoid a disturbance.

When you are grading the exams, consult with the professor and decide on a course of action. Inform the student of your decision; if you are concerned that the student will be belligerent, ask the professor to attend the meeting.

Grading Exams

If you find exams with strikingly similar answers and/or mistakes, you must talk with the students involved. First, tell the professor about the problem if you are leading a discussion section of a larger lecture and ask the professor to attend your meetings with the students. Meet with the students individually. Tell each one that you have found unusual similarities between their exam and another student's and ask them to explain.

Grade Complaints

You can be fairly certain that, at some point along the line (and probably sooner rather than later), you will get a complaint about a paper, an exam, a quiz, or a final grade. There are a few universal reasons for grade complaints.

- Some first-year students who did well in high school may be shocked by their first set of (lower) college grades, and you may bear the brunt of that adjustment period.

- Some students will try to contest a grade just to see if you will change it; they may not believe they deserve a better grade, but they would be more than happy to get one anyway. They think it is at least worth a try.

- Some students will think that they can flirt a teaching assistant into giving them a better grade.

- Some male students will think that they can intimidate a female teaching assistant into giving them a better grade.

- You gave a particularly hard assignment or exam, and many students struggled.

- You give lower grades than another teaching assistant the students may have had.

Keep an open mind when discussing the grade but do not assume that you are wrong. The fact that a student has taken the time to come to office hours to question a grade does not justify a grade change. But naturally, if the error is yours, be gracious about changing the grade. Doing so in no way undermines your authority; stubbornly refusing to recognize a mistake does.

Complaints about a Graded Assignment

When you return graded material, be sure to tell students how the material was graded as well as when and how they should contact you with questions or concerns. If the majority of the grades were low and you expect students may be upset, do not hesitate to tell the class where they had problems and how they can deal with this grade in order to get a better final grade. Always remember that the final grade is a focal point for them and that you are not "coming down a level" to discuss what they need to do in order to get the grade they want. See this instead as an incentive that will make students work harder.

When a student comes to your office hours with a grade complaint, discuss the grade with them calmly and rationally (regardless of their attitude). Do your best to be fair, poised, and authoritative in these situations. Indeed, the most difficult aspect of grade complaints is that students may take their grades very personally and may try to engage you in a discussion about what you have "done" to them. Never meet this approach head-on. Immediately shift the conversation away from being about a problem between you and the student to one about the student and the material. Position yourself as the helpful and informative teacher who is interested in helping the student increase their understanding of the course material.

Regardless of how the student approaches you, treat their grade complaint as a welcomed opportunity to clarify any confusion the student has about how you did your grading, the scoring system in the class, or the course material itself.

DON'T   Immediately jump to the defensive and feel you must list every problem in the graded assignment.

Discuss grades right after class; students need time to digest the grade or your comments (and perhaps write a response).

DO   Ask the student to come to the meeting with a written paragraph explaining what grade they feel would be appropriate for the work so that you can use it as a basis for discussion.

Make the student do most of the talking in a grade complaint situation.

Listen for where the student might have misunderstood the material and offer clarification.

At the beginning of the meeting, ask the student to explain what in your comments they did not understand and why they believe the grade is not appropriate.

Pick out the major problems you addressed in your written comments and ask the student to talk through their response to these criticisms.

Put their grade in the context of the other grades in the class; they may need a reminder that grades are relative and that other students may be doing better work.

Refer them to the criteria you established in the beginning of the course about grades; the clearer the criteria, the easier this situation is to handle.

See pages 127–36 in Chapter 7, Grading Essays, for more on grading criteria.

A Complaint about an Essay Grade

Student: I don't understand why I got a C on this paper. I worked really hard on it.

TA: I know you worked hard on it. Did you understand my comments on the paper?

Student: (looking at the comments): Well, yeah. But I don't see why they make it a C paper. I know the organization could have been a little better, but you said the ideas were all okay.

TA: So if you were going to revise this paper, how would you reorganize it?

Student: (Muddles their way through trying to reorganize their ideas.)

TA: That sounds much better. But as you can see, those are some pretty drastic changes you're going to have to make to clarify your argument. And if you remember on the grading criteria handout, I told you that a B paper can only have minor lapses in organization. Now, did you understand what parts of the paper I was referring to when I wrote that you needed to expand some of these ideas? (And so on.)

A Complaint about an Exam Score

Student: I think you took off too many points on my exam. Why did I lose half the points on Question 6?

TA: You only answered half the question. You needed to provide an explanation for why the mutation happens.

Student: But the question is really confusing and it doesn't really say you have to explain it.

TA: It is a long question, but it does ask you to provide an explanation. Other students in the class did, so it is only fair to give them credit for having done so.

A Complaint about Consistently Poor Grades

> *Student:* You keep giving me bad grades on my papers. And I keep doing what you say, and then you give me another bad grade.
>
> *TA:* I understand how frustrating this is. In part it's because my expectations go up with each paper. You need to fix the problems I comment on, but you also need to push yourself a step farther.
>
> *Student:* But I don't think I'll ever get more than a B.
>
> *TA:* You are very capable of getting a higher grade, but you're really going to have to push yourself to do it. If you remember on the grade-explanation criteria handout, I wrote that an A paper shows innovation or pushes boundaries in some way. That is hard to do, and it involves more than just fixing mechanics.

A Complaint about "Hard Grading"

> *Student:* You graded this test way too hard. My roommate took this course last year and said that if I studied, I would do well. And I studied, and you gave me a C+.
>
> *TA:* I graded the exam as fairly as possible, and there was a wide range of grades in the class. Some students did very well. Remember, your grade is not a reward for hard work. It's a measure of your mastery of the material.

A Belligerent Complaint

Student: I was really surprised to get my final grade for the course. I got a B– when I was expecting an A–.

TA: Here's how I computed your final grade: you got a B on the first paper and a C on the second and third paper. I have you down for an A on the final exam and a B for class participation and attendance.

Student: Why did I get a B for class participation? I talked every day!

TA: You did participate on the days that you were there, but you also had four absences. I outlined clearly in the syllabus that your participation grade would be lowered for every absence past your second.

Student: That's not fair! I had to go to my grandmother's funeral. Did you expect me to miss that for your stupid class?!

TA: Of course not. Unfortunately you already had three other absences when you had to go to her funeral.

Student: I can't believe this, I worked really hard in this class, and you stuck me with a B–, which is now part of my permanent record.

TA: I know that it is disappointing to get a lower grade than you expected, but I graded you and everyone else according to the standards that I set out at the beginning of the semester. I would be happy to adjust your grade if you found that I had miscalculated your points on any assignment or your total points for the semester. Otherwise, your grade stands as it is.

Student: This is unbelievable. You've totally screwed up my transcript, and you won't do anything about it!

TA: Like I said, you will need to show me where I graded you unfairly. Short of that, I cannot change your grade. I'm afraid we're going to have to stop this discussion for today. If you would like to, you can choose to talk with Professor Barry or to meet with the director of undergraduate studies.

Student: That's it?! That's all you'll do?!

TA: Yes, that is all I will do. I have other students to meet with now.

Student storms out of office, muttering obscenities under her breath.

TA, clearly shaken, reassures himself that it is more important to be fair to all of his students than it is to adjust his standard for belligerent students.

Complaints about a Final Grade

Make the student do most of the talking in a conference about a final grade. Remind them that unless you have made a mathematical error in calculating their grade, it is not fair to change their grade and not their classmates' grades. Some students might argue that they need a B+ instead of a B to get into the graduate school of their choice and believe that you can and will change the grade for them. Emphasize to them how unfair this action would be for all the other students in the class.

Some students will ask about their grade on e-mail. Here is an effective formula to follow in your response.

Marvin,

I appreciate your concern about the grade, and I am glad that you asked for clarification. According to my records, you got a B– on the midterm, a B on the final, a C and a B+ on the two papers, and a B+ on the presentation. You were absent four times, and as you were only allowed three absences, that affected your participation grade. Following the grade percentages on the syllabus, I calculated your final grade to be a B. If you have anything different for any of these grades or for the final calculation, please let me know, and I will be happy to discuss changing the final grade. But otherwise, it would not be fair to your classmates, who were graded according to the same criteria, to change your grade. Best of luck in the coming semester.

Tasha

Students with Persistent Complaints

If a student is persistent in their complaints and you are an assistant in a large lecture class, tell the professor about the situation as soon as you see that the problem is not going to be resolved easily. It is the professor's responsibility to support you or help you deal with this kind of situation. It is most helpful for the professor if you keep them apprised of the situation as it develops. Once you have talked with the professor and the student then says, "I am going to go talk to Professor Choi about this grade," you can say,

"That is a good idea. Do you know how to get in touch with her?" This response will take much of the wind out of most students' sails or provide students a recourse if they truly feel the grade is unfair. If you are teaching your own class, alert the director of undergraduate studies to this situation.

If it becomes evident at any point in the semester that a student may complain persistently (and perhaps hostilely) about grades, keep a detailed record of your interactions with the student in case you need it at the end of the semester when it comes to the final grade: photocopy papers with your comments, photocopy exams, take notes on meetings you've had with the student, and so on. You may never need to use this material, but you will be glad to have it if you do.

▣ Helicopter Parents

The last decade has brought to college a generation of students whose parents are more engaged in the day-to-day details of their child's education than parents of years past. While it is difficult to account for the source of this phenomenon (smaller families, the pervasive use of cell phones, a sense of the world being more competitive than ever?), the term *helicopter parent* has emerged to describe parents who hover over their child, even after the child has gone off to college. Most of these parents are well-meaning advocates for their children. However, laws require universities to protect the privacy of every student's academic information, even from the student's parents. Given these laws, in your role as an instructor you must be careful with parents who seek to communicate with you about their child's work in your course.

Responding to the Parent

Often, your first communication with a student's parent will arrive in the form of an email or phone call. Be gracious in your response while making it clear that privacy laws prevent you from sharing information with the parent. Also, ask the parent to encourage their child to bring their concerns to you directly.

EXAMPLE   Dear Mr. Baker,

Thank you for being in touch about Jenny's work in our course. Privacy laws that protect student confidentiality prevent me from being able to share information with you. Please encourage Jenny to come to my office hours or to make an appointment with me; I'm more than happy to talk with her about her concerns.

Sincerely,

Ms. Carmichael

If the parent persists in wanting to communicate with you, graciously repeat your initial statement. Most parents will retreat at this point and, hopefully, send their child your way instead.

Parents Who Become Belligerent

On rare occasions, parents will persist in their efforts to intervene on their child's behalf, sometimes becoming belligerent. In these cases, immediately direct the parent to the instructor for your course and/or the chair of your department.

EXAMPLE   "I understand your concern about Jenny's work in our course, but I am unable to provide you with information. You are free to contact Professor Brewer, the course instructor, or Professor Yang, our department chair, if you would like."

Approaching the Student

It is not always clear where students stand with regard to their parents' hovering behavior. Some students may have asked the parent to advocate on their behalf, some may be utterly at ease with the parent's wish to intervene, and some may be totally unaware (and perhaps would be horrified to learn) that their parent has been in touch with you. Based on your knowledge of the student and their work in your course, use your judgment about whether it makes sense to approach the student about your communication with their parent.

Students who are, indeed, struggling in your course may benefit from some information about how to advocate for themselves. In an email or in person, consider approaching the student.

EXAMPLE   Jenny, as you may know, your dad contacted me today about your work in our course. I am happy to answer any questions you may have and to help you get on firm footing in the course; feel free to stop by my office hours or to make an appointment if my office hours don't work well for you.

Best,

Maya

If the student in question seems to be managing well or chugging along quite happily in your course, you may decide not to approach the student and instead wait for the student to come to you if they are in need of academic guidance or support.

Letters of Recommendation

Because you often teach small classes of students and thereby come to know your students individually, students may regularly come to you for letters of recommendation.

Responding to the Request

When students ask you for letters of recommendation, be honest with them about how comfortable you feel writing such letters. Take every such request under serious consideration before agreeing or not agreeing to write a letter. You do not want to find yourself in the position of writing a letter for a student you cannot comfortably endorse.

GOOD STUDENT   If you know the student well, agree to write the letter with enthusiasm (students often are nervous about asking, and this will reassure them).

Whether or not you know the student well, agree to write the letter but ask for additional materials (e.g., a résumé, a personal statement written for a graduate school application, a writing sample, a paper they wrote for you, etc.).

AVERAGE STUDENT   Decide whether or not you can write a helpful letter. If so, ask for additional materials if you need them. If not, ask the student whether there are other instructors who might be more familiar with their work and academic strengths.

POOR STUDENT   Ask the student whether there are other instructors they can ask—instructors who have seen their best work and perhaps know them better. If you need to, say that you do not think, given what you have seen of the student's work, you could write a helpful letter.

If you find yourself in the middle of trying to write a recommendation and realize that you cannot honestly write a supportive letter, you need to contact that student as soon as possible and advise that they seek out another recommender.

Writing the Letter

If you agree to write a letter, ask for as many details as you can about the position for which the student is applying and why they are applying—in other words, how they are going to use this letter. Ask for statements of purpose or résumés if you wish. The more specific and tailored you can make the letter, the more helpful it will be. Show that you *know* the student and describe unique, outstanding characteristics, if you can. A few hints:

- Include specific details (e.g., an incident in class, a paper the student wrote).

- If you have minor reservations, include those also—they can make the letter more balanced and believable. However, remember that letters of recommendation tend to be "overinflated" across the board. Be extremely careful, therefore, in phrasing these reservations if you do not want the student's application to be adversely affected.

- Describe the student's "extracurricular self" if the student has provided you with information about their activities outside your class.

- Describe the student's work, communication skills, interaction with their peers and with you, goals and their drive to achieve them, improvements student has made, and so on.

- Compare the student's work with that of other students if it will highlight the student's strengths.

Include descriptive details whenever possible but still keep your letter pithy; potential employers and admissions committees want to be able to find the important points of your letter quickly and easily. To this end, front-load the paragraphs with the important points in case the readers do not read the entire paragraph.

Most recommendation forms indicate whether the student has requested a confidential or a non-confidential letter. Bear this in mind when writing the letter.

Ask when the student needs to have the letter mailed, and then meet this deadline. Feel free to ask students to provide you with stamped and addressed envelopes if they have not done so.

Keep electronic versions of all of your letters of recommendation on file. You often will find that you can tailor an old letter of recommendation to fit another student rather than starting from scratch.

See Appendix G for sample letters of recommendation.

■ Further Reading

Davis, B. G. 2009. *Tools for Teaching.* 2d. ed. San Francisco: Jossey-Bass.

Filene, P. 2005. *The Joy of Teaching: A Practical Guide for New College Instructors.* Chapel Hill: University of North Carolina Press.

Hodge, B. M., and J. Preston-Sabin, eds. 1997. *Accommodations—or Just Good Teaching? Strategies for Teaching College Students with Disabilities.* Westport, CT: Praeger.

Kottler, J. 1997. *Succeeding with Difficult Students.* Thousand Oaks, CA: Corwin Press.

Paludi, M. A., ed. 1996. *Sexual Harassment on College Campuses: Abusing the Ivory Power.* Albany: State University of New York Press.

Tice, S.L., N. Jackson, L.M. Lambert, and P. Englot, eds. 2005. *University Teaching: A Reference Guide for Graduate Students and Faculty.* 2nd ed. Syracuse, NY: Syracuse University Press.

9

Feedback from Students

Feedback from students, while it can be rewarding, also can be one of the more frightening parts of teaching. A good student is one who seeks out feedback, listens to it, and uses that knowledge to improve their performance. The same holds true for a good instructor. And while it can be stressful to ask students for feedback about the class, it is better for you to know their responses along the way rather than to wait until the end of term. Also, remember that in the same way paper grades are about the student's work—not about the student—student feedback is about the course, not about your value as a person. This chapter will discuss ways to make student feedback as useful and constructive as possible.

▨ Encouraging Feedback from Students

At the beginning of the semester, tell your students that you would like them to keep you informed of their thoughts about the course throughout the term. Feedback always needs to be a two-way street. Encourage them to share their thoughts about the assignments, course discussions, lectures, readings, lab experiments, and class format. Sometimes it can feel like open-firing season when you create this space for feedback but remember you feel no more vulnerable than the students do when they turn in a paper to be graded.

Do not view this as a time to share your own anxieties about the course or to apologize for inexperience, workload, and so on. Simply tell students that you are interested in their feedback so that you can be sure they are learning effectively. This move (and your willingness to make it) will reinforce your authority in the classroom.

How Students Should Contact You

Let students know how they can give you feedback about aspects of the course. You might encourage them to use email, to drop a note in your box in the department, to stop by your office hours, or to bend your ear after class. If you would like students to be able to give you anonymous feedback, be sure there is a place where they can leave written notes for you throughout the semester.

Eliciting Informal Feedback from Students

It is not enough for you to tell students that you would like their feedback and to make the routes of communication available. You also need to solicit specific feedback throughout the semester.

In-Class Activities

In-class questions obviously provide the most frequent and direct form of student feedback. You can also elicit feedback about how well students understand the material using one of these "mini" lesson plans.

Sample Precinct

Choose a "sample precinct" (a row or a cluster of students). Admit that you are going to put them on the spot by asking them all a series of questions, but make it clear that they are just the sample group. You are using these questions to assess overall class understanding, not to highlight their shortcomings and/or brilliance. Choose different precincts over the course of the term.

Initial Freewriting Activity

Ask students to take a few minutes at the beginning of class to write what they recall from the last lecture or what they found confusing in the reading. Then ask for volunteers to share one of their responses; you can keep a list of the responses on the board. This activity can help provide continuity between lecture and section and help you focus your teaching on problem areas.

Final Freewriting Activity

Ask students to take a few minutes at the end of class to respond in writing to a question you ask. Depending on the question, you can make these responses anonymous or not.

    EXAMPLES "Tell me what you now know about derivatives."

               "Summarize for me what we talked about in class today."

               "What concept is feeling the most confusing to you right now?"

               "If we could review two things in class on Wednesday, what would they be?"

You can then use these answers to give students feedback about their progress or concerns as a class and to focus your teaching in the next class. Always read what they have written, but do not feel compelled to respond individually (in writing or orally) to each student.

Responses to Your Written Comments

Some teaching assistants have had success asking students to respond in writing to the teaching assistant's comments on a given essay or other assignment. If nothing else, this forces students to read the comments, and, at best, it helps them to process the critique and ask questions about comments that they do not understand. It can be a time-consuming process but often a worthwhile one.

If all your students have email, you can require them to email you within 24 or 48 hours with a paragraph response to your comments on their paper. In this way, you open up a dialogue about the paper and their writing. Be sure to give them some guidelines (e.g., they must ask at least one question or describe their plan for revision), or else you may get mostly praise for your insight (a.k.a. brownnosing in hopes that the next grade you give them will be better).

You also can ask students to write responses below yours on the papers themselves and turn them in at the next class meeting.

You then will briefly respond to their comments and return the papers at the following meeting. You probably will want to keep notes in your files on their responses or ask them to turn in all previous work with each assignment so that you can target your comments more effectively on the next graded assignment.

Responding to Informal Student Feedback

If you solicit feedback from your students, you must respond to it. Two strategies for responding follow.

Adjusting Your Lesson Plan

If a consistent pattern emerges in the students' feedback that indicates areas of ongoing confusion, you need to take the time to review that material or, at the very least, provide students with further resources. Particularly in courses that build sequentially, it is imperative that you address gaps in students' understanding before proceeding. If you sense that only some students in the course are struggling with a concept, consider offering a review session on that concept outside of class. A review session can be more efficient than helping students individually in office hours, and it shows students that you are committed to helping them master the course material, even if it takes them a bit longer than some other students.

Meta-Teaching

We use the term *meta-teaching* to refer to talking with your students about the teaching in your course in order to improve their learning. For example, if you felt that the last class meeting was marked by an unusually stilted discussion, ask your students to help you figure out why. While you may have to set aside your pride and admit that your class is no longer going as perfectly as planned, these are almost always fruitful discussions. In broaching the topic, you are reassuring your students that a bad class is not all their responsibility. It puts all of you on the "same team" in figuring out what might have stifled discussion and what can be done to improve the class dynamics.

EXAMPLE   "Last week we talked about the role of the voter in dictating international policy. Many of you seemed confused about how this discussion was relevant to the course. How can we relate it to the larger goals and topics of the course? What could we, or I, have done differently to facilitate a broader consideration of that topic?"

Some teaching assistants worry that meta-teaching will undermine their authority. In fact, the ability to use meta-teaching can demonstrate comfort with your authority in the classroom. Students respect teachers who are aware of and willing to address obvious problems.

DON'T   Use meta-teaching as a way of displacing responsibility for the success of the class (e.g. "I don't understand why you all won't talk in section. I've never had a group as uninterested as yours.").

DO   Use meta-teaching when it will be educational for the students to talk about what is happening in the classroom (e.g., "What does it mean that on Monday you all seemed uncomfortable talking about discrepancies in SAT scores along race and gender lines?").

DON'T   Use meta-teaching to make the course about your insecurities or frustration with teaching; students should feel they are taking a well-planned course, not that they are part of an ongoing experiment (e.g., "I think I've figured out how to make all the groups more talkative. Last week I tried . . .").

DO   Use meta-teaching to address issues that seem to be particular to the material or to the students taking the class (e.g., recognize the complexity of a concept before trying to explain it, respond to unusually low exam grades).

> Use meta-teaching to help students understand lesson plans and how they fit into the broader structure of the course (e.g., "In the last class, we talked about Kant's theories generally as a class. Today I'd like to begin by breaking you into smaller groups and having you dive into the text itself to look at the language Kant uses. I will give you some questions . . .").
>
> Use meta-teaching freely.

You do not have to wait for a difficult discussion to use meta-teaching. The more that both you and your students participate in and reflect on the teaching process as it unfolds, the more you will be able to involve students in learning. While it may feel a bit awkward for you and your students at first, feel free to recognize explicitly many of the dynamics of the class. Do not hesitate to introduce difficult material as difficult and challenge students to rise to the occasion. Do not hesitate to tell students when you are trying a new kind of class activity for them. Do not hesitate to recognize that a discussion may be sensitive or that students may be disappointed with their grades on a given assignment. As a general rule, you can legitimately and effectively give yourself the option of talking about and asking students about what they think is happening in the room as it is happening.

Formal Feedback from Students

Student conferences and written evaluations are ways to ensure that you will get student feedback. They can be very helpful for your teaching if you set them up effectively. If you will be using evaluations in the course, tell your students at the beginning of the semester; then they can prepare thoughtful feedback as the course progresses.

Midterm Conferences

Midterm can be a useful time to meet with each student individually to discuss their progress in the class and to get their feedback on the course. Bring a sign-up sheet to class with appointments scheduled 15 or 20 minutes apart for each student to sign up for a convenient time.

At the conference, you need to be prepared with topics to discuss or to have asked students to prepare topics; you have asked the students to come see you, so you must try to make the conference productive. You can have notes ready on each student's work in the class and prepare a few questions to ask them about their experience in the class so far; these questions can be similar to those on a written midterm evaluation.

Written Midterm Feedback

Written midterm feedback is remarkably helpful in running a successful class or section. The feedback form can be fairly short (a half page, taking only ten minutes of class time); it still allows students to have some say in the content and direction of the course. Very few instructors ask their students what *they* want in a course, and students are generally appreciative and constructive when given this opportunity. These forms should be anonymous.

Writing the Questions

Ask questions that encourage students to be honest and take an active part in the shape of the course. Ask open-ended questions that require a response longer than yes or no. You probably do not need more than four or five questions.

EXAMPLES "I would like to see more/less time spent on

_____."

"In the second half of the term, I would like to talk about _____."

"Written comments on my paper would be more helpful if _____"

> See Appendix H for sample midterm feedback forms.

Preparing the Students

Many students do not focus on the fact that you are going to read these feedback forms and that you have feelings too. Before you hand out forms, you may want to tell students that you will be reading them and that you take them seriously. Also tell them that you would appreciate all suggestions and any constructive feedback they wish to provide. To encourage them to be honest, try to time the evaluation so that you are not holding papers or exams at the time. You do not want to "butter them up" so that they will only praise you and the course—you need to hear about what can be improved. But it is fair to remind students that you, a fellow human being, will be reading their comments so that they focus on being constructive instead of destructive if they have concerns to voice.

Talking about the Feedback

You must be sure to talk briefly about the feedback in the next class after you have read the forms. The students need to hear you respond to their concerns and suggestions.

EXAMPLES "Many of you said that you found it useful when I put an outline of the lecture on the board, so I will try to do that consistently."

"A few students commented that we need to slow down when going over problems on the homework. I will try to ask if we're all on the same page as we go, but please let me know if I'm going too fast."

"A couple of students wrote that they wanted to read more poetry. I'm afraid that I cannot work extra reading into the syllabus, but I would be happy to give any of you recommendations on outside reading if you're interested."

Written Final Evaluations

Standardized Evaluations

At almost all universities, students have to fill out a standardized evaluation form for all classes at the end of the term. Many of these ask students to rate aspects of the course and the instructor on a numerical scale. There are pedagogical and administrative reasons for numerical ratings, and you will learn from these scores, but they don't always give you as much detail as you need to substantively improve your teaching approach or the course. Tell students that you are looking for written feedback specific to your course, and you would appreciate it if they took the time to write comments in the space provided on the evaluation. Providing specific questions for students to answer can productively guide student feedback and make it more likely that they will (a) write comments and (b) write comments that will help you refine the teaching of your course.

Supplemental Evaluations

If it is at all feasible, you should write your own evaluation form to enhance the standardized process. Such an evaluation will be particularly useful if you will be teaching the same or a similar course again. Write questions similar to those on the midterm evaluation.

Reading Your Evaluations

Prepare yourself for the fact that reading evaluations can be anywhere from exhilarating to devastating—or both. There almost always will be some negative evaluations in the stack (often from students not doing well in the course), and any number of positive evaluations does little to ease the immediate sting of a student's criticisms. Students may even bypass the course content and go straight for your feelings; students have been known to tell instructors to get new haircuts, buy new clothes, and/or "get a life." These students are usually venting academic frustration in destructive ways; do not let their anger make you question your teaching abilities.

However, you should take consistent negative feedback on a particular aspect of the course very seriously. While your feelings may be hurt, you need to use the students' comments as a way to improve your teaching and/or the course.

Here are a few ways to keep the negative evaluations in perspective.

- Reread the positive ones, and remember that not every student is going to like your course or teaching style.

- Tell a friend or family member about the bad ones so that they can reassure you that these evaluations happen to everyone and that you are still a wonderful person, even if parts of your teaching need to be improved.

- Remember that one course does not make or break your teaching career. Learning to teach effectively is an ongoing process, and there is no reason to expect yourself to be perfect every step of the way.

- Try to see the negative but constructive comments in the perspective of the comments that you write on students' work. You are trying to help them improve and do not intend the comments to be hurtful or personal.

- Remember that even the best teachers have had students criticize their teaching, their grading, their clothes, and even their hairstyles!

Before reading the evaluations, set up your day appropriately.

DON'T Read them right before teaching or even going to a class of your own.

DO Read them in the comfort of your home or with a friend, if you want moral support.

Read them with a cup of your favorite coffee, a bag of chips, or a box of cookies, depending on your comfort food of choice.

Read them.

Read your evaluations because you will learn a lot, and you will improve the course. But be nice to yourself too.

"When I got back my evaluations after my first semester of teaching, I ripped open the envelope and started reading. I read through 21 fine, good, and even wonderful evaluations, and then I got to the last one: there were low scores in every category, and on the back, the student had written, 'I think Joanna is annoying. And it would help if she understood the material.' I was devastated. And I couldn't imagine how I was going to walk into the classroom and start teaching . . . in five minutes!"

Further Reading

Angelo, T. A., and K. P. Cross. 1993. *Classroom Assessment Techniques: A Handbook for College Teachers.* 2d ed. San Francisco: Jossey-Bass.

Brookfield, S. D. 2006. *The Skillful Teacher: On Technique, Trust, and Responsiveness in the Classroom.* 2d ed. San Francisco: Jossey-Bass.

Davis, B. G. 2009. *Tools for Teaching.* 2d. ed. San Francisco: Jossey-Bass.

Lowman, J. 1995. *Mastering the Techniques of Teaching.* 2d ed. San Francisco: Jossey-Bass.

Svinicki, M., and W. J. McKeachie. 2011. *McKeachie's Teaching Tips: Strategies, Research, and Theory for College and University Teachers.* 13th ed. Belmont, CA: Wadsworth.

Preparing for the Job Market

As you wrap up your graduate career and consider professional positions that involve teaching at the college level, you will probably be asked to demonstrate your teaching credentials as part of the job search process. Schools may ask you to send "evidence of teaching excellence" or "a teaching portfolio." What do you send? They may also ask to interview you. What do you say? This chapter describes how to begin preparing the professional portfolio that will demonstrate your skills and experience as a teacher as well as how to prepare for teaching questions in an interview.

▣ The Teaching Portfolio: A Few Basics

There is no complete consensus about exactly what goes into a teaching portfolio, and in all honesty, some job search committees that ask for "evidence of teaching excellence" may not be entirely sure what they expect you to send. The sections that follow describe a typical structure of a teaching portfolio, which you can adapt to your field and a particular job. The key is to present the portfolio professionally, as this speaks to your seriousness about teaching as a professional pursuit and demonstrates organizational and other skills that you bring to your teaching.

Typical Structure

The portfolio should be neat and well organized, free of typos and coffee stains. In other words, it should look professional. For example, even if all your assignments for a course were not formatted consistently for the actual course, you probably want to make them consistent for the portfolio. Create a cover page with your name, institution, and the date.

A teaching portfolio often contains five major categories of materials, after the cover page and table of contents:

Cover page

Table of Contents

1. A statement of teaching philosophy

2. Description of courses taught (perhaps preceded by a list of courses taught)

3. Sample syllabi

4. Sample course materials (e.g., essay assignments, PowerPoint slides, handouts, exams, sample student work with your feedback)

5. Teaching evaluations

   a. from students

   b. from peers/supervisors

Detailed information is provided about each category of material in the section that follows, but first, here are a couple of key pieces of advice.

Getting Started

You can't start too early gathering materials for your teaching portfolio. When you start teaching as a graduate student, it may feel like you have lots of time before you will need to put together evidence of your teaching for the job market. But time flies, and it is much more fun to put together a portfolio by selecting from among your beautifully organized files of teaching materials than by scrambling around trying to find or create good teaching materials.

DON'T   Put your teaching materials in miscellaneous folders with labels that do not make clear what is in a document or file.

DO   Keep neat, organized files (electronic and/or paper) of teaching materials for every course.

DON'T   Find yourself surfing the Internet trying to locate a student who graduated two years ago, because she wrote a really interesting paper for a given assignment and you want to get permission to include it in your portfolio.

DO   Ask students during the term for permission to use their work for professional or teaching purposes if you think their work effectively exemplifies your teaching.

> See pages 216–17 in this chapter, Student Work, for more information on getting permission from students to use their work.

DON'T   Wait until your last year in graduate school, when you are on fellowship and not teaching, to ask a faculty member for a letter that evaluates your teaching.

DO   Ask your advisor or another faculty member to come observe your teaching early and more than once, if possible, so that they can write you a letter.

> See pages 217–19 in this chapter, Evaluations, for more information about acquiring such a letter.

Working with What You've Got

It can be intimidating to put together a teaching portfolio if you haven't had much experience teaching or if all your teaching has been leading discussion sections for larger courses that you did not design. If you have less experience designing and teaching your own course, you will want to think about what you have learned from (a) leading discussion sections or labs and (b) observing someone else design and teach a course. We can learn a lot about how we want to teach from working with a course we didn't plan, especially if we make ourselves figure out why we would and would not implement specific aspects of that course's design.

Teaching portfolios can include not only materials that you have already designed for courses (handouts, essay prompts) but also "dream" materials that you would create to teach a specific concept or course. A portfolio is designed to capture your potential as a teacher, whether or not you have yet had the opportunity to implement all of these ideas in a classroom.

Enjoying the Benefits

One fundamental purpose of a teaching portfolio is to provide evidence of your teaching abilities and experience as you apply for jobs, awards, and other professional opportunities. But teaching portfolios also help make us more self-reflective teachers by asking us to organize and explicate our materials across courses, to articulate why and how we plan our courses, to collect and learn from student and peer feedback, and to explain what motivates our teaching practices. As we become more able to explain these things to ourselves and our colleagues, we usually become better at being clear—and more willing to be explicitly clear—with students about why we are doing what we are doing in our classes. This makes us better teachers. Knowing that you may be compiling a teaching portfolio may also inspire you to create exemplary materials for your courses/sections.

■ A Teaching Philosophy

A teaching philosophy puts forward your fundamental approach(es) to teaching—both teaching material in your field and teaching more generally. It articulates the principles and goals that guide your course design and classroom practice. It captures what motivates you as a teacher and how you motivate your students. Sound hard to do? It is.

Teaching philosophies are extremely difficult to write. You will probably draft your philosophy, read it, and think it sounds stupid. Or trite. Or both. Most serious teachers have written dozens of drafts of their teaching philosophies and continue to revise their philosophies over their entire careers. As you revise, you will find the core principles that drive your teaching and have the pleasure of watching them develop as you continue to learn from teaching.

Format

Teaching philosophies are typically one or two single-spaced pages. Even if you are long-winded, aim to keep your philosophy under two pages. Lengthy philosophies, in all likelihood, are talking more about teaching practice than teaching philosophy.

Content

Remember you are crafting a statement of teaching philosophy and not of teaching practice; your philosophy needs to drive the structure of the statement. You should include descriptions of practice as supporting evidence for how parts of your philosophy play out in your teaching. In this way, a teaching philosophy is like any other good piece of writing: lively, detailed supporting examples make the larger claims more persuasive. Your teaching philosophy should reflect your approach to teaching more broadly as an enterprise and also be grounded in pedagogical approaches and content specific to your discipline.

Here are some questions to help you figure out the teaching philosophy that motivates your teaching:

- What are the goals that guide your courses and your lesson plans? (Think particularly about goals that underlie any content specific to a given course.)
- How do you think about teaching and learning?
- What is the rationale for the specific assignments/learning assessments that you have assigned or would assign?
- What do you want students to remember or be able to do a year after they take your course?

- When you think about the best moments in your teaching, what has made them so rewarding?
- What kind of interaction do you strive to encourage in the classroom, and why?
- How has your pedagogy developed?
- What draws you to the profession of teaching?

> **"The first teaching philosophy I ever wrote was for a teaching award. It was five pages—and it was all practice! 'I use small group work . . . I learn all their names . . . I use clickers to encourage participation.' I had no idea what I was doing. I can only imagine what the committee thought while they were reading it, but I do know that was a teaching award I did not receive!"**

Remember that, fundamentally, teaching is about learning. Thinking about how you conceptualize learning and what kind of learning you are trying to foster in your classes will help you articulate your teaching philosophy.

EXAMPLES   A teaching philosophy in physics may focus more on the types of problem-solving skills and the general principles that you hope students will acquire than on content more specific to a given course.

A teaching philosophy in English may focus on particular approaches to reading literary texts and to writing arguments rather than discussion of mastery of specific literary works.

Specific Advice

Once you have drafted your philosophy, here are a few useful hints to consider as you revise.

DON'T Make your teaching philosophy all about you.

DO   Make students a central part of your teaching philosophy. (Hint: Calculate a ratio of how many times you mention yourself compared with your students. This may help you see parts of the philosophy you want to revise.)

DON'T Rely on clichéd descriptions of good teaching such as "active learning" or "creating a sense of community" with no further explanation.

DO   Interrogate the clichéd descriptions of good teaching that you believe in (there is a reason that they have become cliché!) to figure out what they actually mean to you and your teaching; then explain in your philosophy how these play out in your teaching.

DON'T List teaching practices, even if you create beautiful transitions in between.

DO   Use effective examples of specific teaching practices to support your descriptions of components of your teaching philosophy.

DON'T Say anything that could be read as condescending toward or negative about students.

DO   Be respectful of students in terms of what they bring to the classroom and the learning process.

DON'T Refer to scholarship on teaching just to refer to scholarship on teaching.

DO   Refer to scholarship on teaching if it has genuinely shaped how you teach.

DON'T Edit out language that you feel actually does describe how you think about teaching because you are worried it is too trite, too humorous, or too genuine.

DO   Be true to who you are as a teacher and how you think about teaching and learning.

We strongly recommend that you ask advanced graduate students and faculty in your discipline for sample teaching philosophies as well.

> **"In the evaluations of my first courses, student after student wrote that I assigned too much reading. I was so ambitious about what we could cover. In my teaching philosophy, I write about how I learned from this experience that less is more, and how it has shaped my teaching ever since."**

■ Sample Teaching Materials

Many of the sample materials in your teaching portfolio will be materials from courses that you have taught. However, you are allowed to revise these materials; they do not need to be identical to the version you used in the course if you think they could be improved. You can also include "dream materials" for courses that you hope to teach at some point. All these materials allow others to see and evaluate how you do or would teach a particular course, which is the purpose of the portfolio.

Sample Syllabi

Choose your favorite syllabi. Typically a course portfolio will contain between two and four syllabi. Try to show range (in the content of the courses and in course level/size) and your ability to frame a course. As noted, you can revise ones you have and/or include a syllabus for a course that you have not taught yet. You may be asked in an interview about a "dream course," so it can be useful to create the syllabus for that course—and if you like it, you should put it in your teaching portfolio.

Sample Assignments and Materials

For this section of the teaching portfolio, it can be helpful to provide an introductory page that frames the assignments and/or materials. On this page, you can explain what course(s) the materials are for, the goals of the assignments/handouts, how the assignment/handout sequence progresses (if relevant), etc. Typical sample materials include essay assignments (including a partial or full assignment sequence, if relevant to your course) or class handouts about content specific to a course, exams, and/or PowerPoint slides from a lecture. You can also include in this section materials you use to structure class discussion or informal written responses, if you think they usefully showcase particular aspects of your teaching. With all the materials, consider how they speak to the goals of a course and what innovative and/or effective aspects of your pedagogy they capture. Typically, this section will be 8–20 pages.

DON'T Overwhelm your readers with materials from every course you have taught.

Do Select an assignment sequence and/or a set of handouts that will speak effectively to your teaching approach and abilities.

DON'T Expect your sample teaching materials to be self-explanatory.

Do Provide some context and framing on the introductory page so that readers understand why you have included these specific materials.

Some instructors will include a video of themselves teaching in the portfolio. Most committees will not expect such a video. But if you have a video that shows you teaching effectively (and your friends agree that this is the case), then consider including it in your portfolio.

Student Work

Many portfolios don't include actual examples of student work, and it can be risky to include such materials: not all committee members may agree with your assessment of the work and they will be seeing your feedback on the work without much context. That said, in some fields, including student work can effectively exemplify your teaching. For example, providing a student paper with your comments in the margins and your endnote to the student can show readers how you respond to and evaluate student work. While it certainly can feel like it speaks volumes about our teaching to include an A paper or other assignment to show the excellence our students achieve, it often shows more about your teaching to include B-level work and your feedback on it. B-level work can capture both what students are learning and where they are encountering challenges, which allows you to showcase how you affirm what they are doing well and help them address the areas where they are still struggling.

In general, it is a good idea to collect samples of student work in any term, both for your teaching portfolio and for use as models for future students. To do this, you need to get permission from the student to use their work for future teaching and/or professional purposes. Check with your department or school to find out if there is a standard consent form. If not, you will need to determine if there are any institutional guidelines for collecting student work. Most consent forms contain details about the course and the semester, a statement from the student giving you permission to use the work for teaching and/or professional purposes, and the option to have the work be used anonymously or with their name.

> See Appendix I for a sample coursework release form.

Evaluations

This section of the teaching portfolio allows readers to see how students and colleagues have evaluated your teaching. As with the teaching materials section, this section also only provides samples. In other words, this does not have to be a confessional with any and every comment you have ever received from a student. That said, it should be representative of your teaching—although it can and should certainly highlight your most effective teaching.

Numerical Scores

If your institution provides summary sheets with your overall scores for courses, along with the questions, include a selection of these. You do not have to include all of your summary sheets unless a school asks you to do so. If possible, you want to show range here, across different courses and over time. It can be helpful to include an introductory page that explains the point system, as well as which evaluations you have included (e.g., if they include discussion sections).

Student Comments

The challenge here is including student comments without overwhelming your readers with reams of paper. Most instructors, for example, will select student comments from only a couple of courses to include with the numerical summary sheets. So you may be providing numerical summary sheets for some courses without the specific comments from students.

In terms of presenting the comments themselves, here are a couple of options:

- If your institution has moved to a form of electronic evaluation that provides a summary of student comments in a condensed form, you can include this document as is.
- If student comments come on an individual piece of paper for every student, you can:
  - include selected sheets (and include a note about the basis of selection);
  - retype selected student comments into a new document (e.g., as a bulleted list). With a smaller class, you can include most if not all of the comments, and with a bigger class, you should try to capture themes. Your readers will work from the premise that you are a trustworthy transcriber, and you should earn their trust. That said, if you have one off-the-wall mean comment in a set of 40 comments, you do not necessarily have to include that; it is fair to say that it is not representative.

Your readers are looking to see, at least in part, if you have taught successful courses. All teachers can have a course or a semester that does not go exactly as they hoped it would. A teaching portfolio aims to show what you are capable of as a teacher.

Remember also that teaching success takes many forms, only one of which is high evaluation scores. If you have been struggling with lower evaluation scores, you can use the portfolio to demonstrate the quality of your materials, your thoughtfulness about course design, and your reflectiveness—particularly in the teaching portfolio—about what you have learned from the feedback you have received from students.

Letter from a Teaching Supervisor, Advisor, or Peer

It can be effective to include an observation/evaluation from a teaching supervisor, advisor, or peer. As part of the overall job application process, you may also have a confidential letter of recommendation that addresses your teaching that comes under separate cover. But if possible, a detailed observation/evaluation in your portfolio is a useful complement to student evaluations. So when you are teaching a course that you think is going well, invite your supervisor, a graduate student mentor, or a committee member to visit your class. Be sure to ask them ahead of time if they would be willing to write up the visit for these purposes.

> "Every term, a certain number of students say (complain!) that the course involves a lot of work. I included comments along those lines when I typed up selected student comments. I mean, it is representative. But also, it is part of my teaching. I do ask for a lot from students—but I know they learn a lot in my courses too."

■ Electronic Teaching Portfolios

Putting your teaching portfolio online can allow you to exploit (a) hypertext links in terms of organizing the materials and (b) the additional space that the Internet allows (no tree-killing involved). For now you probably want to have a hard copy version that you can send as well, as some job search committees may prefer hard copy. You can always provide a link in the hard copy version to additional materials available online.

Remember that an electronic teaching portfolio is not just a paper portfolio turned into a PDF and put online. Viewers will expect your portfolio to use links and potentially images in at least relatively sophisticated ways. Your ability to create this kind of electronic portfolio will be seen as another asset in your teaching repertoire.

▣ Job Interviews

Most interviews for jobs in academia will involve questions about teaching. And to some extent, interviewers will be using all of the interview to assess how good they think you would be in a classroom (based on your enthusiasm about the material, your ability to respond to questions, etc.). Luckily, there are many ways to prepare yourself for teaching questions. Your skills as a teacher will also serve you very well in an interview. Just think: every time you teach, you successfully field questions you were not expecting.

Preparing for the Interview

Odds are that you will be asked how you would teach particular courses, so it can be useful to sketch out a preliminary syllabus for some standard courses in your field ahead of time. In addition, sketch out your dream course because you may be asked about that as well. You don't need to have a week-by-week schedule for these courses, but you should think about the course goals, the overarching structure of the course, the course texts, and some possible assignments.

Make a list of five or six things that you want to make sure that the interview committee knows by the time you leave the interview. This can help you feel like you have some control over the interview (which you do) and ensure that the committee knows about your strengths. You will find that you can use the material on this list in answers to a wide range of questions.

Do your homework about the school at which you are interviewing. This way, you will have a sense of the mission of the department, what kinds of courses you might be expected to teach, and what you might like to ask during the interview. A committee may read your lack of familiarity with readily available information about the school/department as indicating your less than serious interest in the job.

Interview Questions

You will undoubtedly get questions that none of us could have anticipated, but here is a list of some typical interview questions about teaching:

- How would you approach teaching _____ course?
- We have a senior seminar and faculty can focus it on the topic of their choosing. What would you teach?
- What do you find is the biggest challenge students encounter in your courses? How do you help them with this challenge?
- What has been one of your most rewarding teaching moments and why?
- What has been one of your most challenging teaching moments, and how did you handle it?
- Could you teach _____ course?
- What do you see as one of your most effective teaching strategies?
- What do you see as your weaknesses as a teacher, and how have you addressed those?
- How do you incorporate new technology into your teaching?
- How do you assess student learning in your courses?
- How has your teaching changed over time?

There is obviously no one right answer to any of these questions. But we can offer some general advice about how to approach these questions.

DON'T   Simply list the information units or texts that you would cover, in response to a question about how you would teach a course.

DO   Describe how you would teach a course, start by framing the course in terms of your goals for the students and the course's overarching structure. You can then provide a few examples of information units or texts you would cover.

DON'T Describe a dream course that focuses on your dissertation topic.

Do   Use the question about a dream course to show your range as a teacher and your ability to teach exciting new courses outside the area of your dissertation research.

DON'T Say no to any question about whether you could teach a course in an area that is close to what it is reasonable to expect you to teach.

Do   Say, "Yes, I would be interested in teaching that course" even with courses you are not sure how you would teach. If the course is far afield for you, you can say that you would need a summer to prepare. Saying yes shows your willingness to be a good citizen of a department and to take on new teaching challenges.

DON'T Feel you have to answer a question immediately if you don't understand it or don't have enough information yet to answer it.

Do   Feel free to ask follow-up questions (e.g., Is there a prerequisite for that course? What level of students typically take that course?). These kinds of questions can demonstrate your thoughtfulness as well as your awareness of what it means to teach within a larger curriculum.

DON'T Say you have no teaching weaknesses.

Do   Use feedback you have received from students to frame something that you have been working to improve in your teaching.

DON'T Answer all the teaching questions in broad strokes and feel like you need to contain excitement you feel about teaching.

Do   Use specific anecdotes from your teaching experience to capture strategies you use effectively in your teaching as well as to convey your enthusiasm for teaching.

The interview itself is a wonderful opportunity for you to demonstrate your teaching skills, from answering questions thoughtfully and explaining material clearly to conveying your enthusiasm to your audience. So while the interview context may be new, you can draw successfully on a set of skills that you have been honing in your classroom.

Further Reading

Barnes, S. L. 2007. *On the Market: Strategies for a Successful Academic Job Search.* Boulder, CO: Lynne Rienner Publishers

Cahn, S. M. 2008. *From Student to Scholar: A Candid Guide to Becoming a Professor.* New York: Columbia University Press.

Murray, John P. 1995. *Successful Faculty Development and Evaluation: The Complete Teaching Portfolio.* ASHE-ERIC Higher Education Report No. 8. Washington, DC: The George Washington University, Graduate School of Education and Human Development.

Vick, J.M., and Furlong, J.S. 2008. *The Academic Job Search Handbook.* 4th ed. Philadelphia: University of Pennsylvania Press.

Relevant Websites

http://taproject.rutgers.edu/services_tips/teach_portfolio.pdf

www.cs.tufts.edu/~ablumer/portfolio.html

www.umass.edu/cft/publications/teachingportfolio.pdf

www.brown.edu/Administration/Sheridan_Center/docs/teach_port.pdf

The Balance of School and Teaching

One of the hardest parts of graduate school is balancing your duties to your students and your duties to yourself and your own education. Most graduate students feel that they could work full-time on any one of their multiple obligations and still not get as much accomplished as they would like. This chapter suggests ways to integrate teaching into your demanding graduate program.

◼ Front-Loading Effort

The better prepared you are for the course at the beginning of the semester, the less work you will have during the semester. If you have control over the syllabus, write a detailed one that guides you from week to week. In addition, take advantage of the lull in your own course work at the beginning of the semester to run lab experiments, to make copies of long handouts, or to complete other foreseeable time-consuming tasks.

◼ Assigning Responsibility

Your job as a teaching assistant is to guide the learning of your students, not to do their work for them. While you should recognize that college course work can be demanding for many students, you should not feel obligated to tailor an individual course of study for each of your students. Ironically, the students who demand the most of your time are often the students who put the least effort into the course. Resolve that you will not do more work for a student than the student is doing for your course.

Here are a few ways to make sure that you do not take too much responsibility and that your students take enough.

- Write a clear and complete syllabus.

Use it as a way to tell students what you will do for them and what they are expected to do for the course. Establish clear guidelines for what will happen when students fail to do their work and stick to them.

DON'T	"Late work will be penalized."
DO	"Paper grades will be lowered by five points for every day late."
DON'T	Assume that every student will feel they have to come to every exam.
DO	"Contact me in advance if you will not be able to attend an exam and need to arrange a makeup. If you do not attend an exam and do not contact me in advance, you will need to provide proof of an emergency in order to take a makeup."

> See pages 16–19 in Chapter 2, Establishing Contact, and pages 20–22 in Chapter 2, Syllabus: Setting the Agenda, for more information on developing your syllabus.

- If a student is struggling in your course, be clear with the student about what *they* must do to get back on track.

DON'T	If a student has missed three weeks of class, offer to meet with them individually to summarize the material.
DO	If a student has missed three weeks of class, explain where the information can be found (the course pack, a friend's notes, etc.) and offer to answer specific questions once they have read over the material.
DON'T	Devise a complex plan for how a student can make up missed work.

Do   Ask the student how they feel they should make up the missed work. They will invariably devise a more demanding and cruel plan than anything you would ever have come up with!

Student: I was in Florida over spring break, and I got so badly sunburned that I haven't been able to come to class for three weeks. What did I miss, and how can I make it up?

TA: Sorry about the burn. In the last three weeks, we have covered Chapters 5 through 10 in the text, the middle third of the course pack, and we have taken two in-class quizzes.

Student: Wow, I missed a lot. What can I do to make it up?

TA: You're right: that is a lot. What do you think would be a good way for you to get completely caught up with the material?

Student: I guess that I could copy a friend's notes, write brief summaries of all the chapters and articles, and write a short paper that covered the material on the quizzes. Does that sound okay?

TA: That sounds fine. Show me the chapter and article summaries and give me the paper to grade. I'll give you two weeks from today to hand them in.

- Schedule your office hours so that they have a defined ending.

You are not obligated to meet with students past the time of your scheduled office hours if you do not want to. Do not hesitate to point out to the student kindly that office hours are ending; do not feel that you need to justify doing so. Invite the student to come to your next scheduled office hours should they wish to do so.

■ Scheduling Teaching-Related Activities

Teaching Classes

You may not have a choice about when you teach your classes. But you may have the option of meeting with all of your classes on one day or of spreading the classes throughout the week. Whatever you choose to do, try to schedule your sections so that they all occur after the same lecture. This way, you need to create only one lesson plan per week. Many teaching assistants prefer to teach all of their classes on the same day, and there are both pros and cons for doing so.

PROS   You will save time by only needing to assemble your teaching materials once each week.

You can get into a "teaching mode" and stay there as you move from one class to the next.

You can make small changes and correct mistakes you see in the class plan.

You can minimize "downtime," as many teaching assistants find that they are not able to do much of their own work right before or right after they teach.

CONS   Teaching can be exhausting, so you may run out of energy before you get to your last class.

If you find that you are missing necessary materials, or that you need to develop a different class plan altogether, you will not have time to make major adjustments before you get to your next class.

A bad first class may affect how you feel about teaching later ones.

Preparing for Class

Be sure to set aside time each week just for teaching preparation. You probably will want to do this at least a couple of days before the class so that you will have time to get any needed materials or to photocopy any handouts. Schedule this time in your planner; it is more efficient and less stressful than trying to cram your preparation in around the edges of your other work. If you want your students to prepare before they come to your class, be sure to get one or two weeks ahead in your class planning so that you can tell them what will be expected week to week.

Making Your Schedule

When you choose to block out preparation and grading time in your schedule will depend on how you function both as a teacher and as a student. A few suggestions:

- Figure out when you do your most productive academic work (be it early in the morning or after midnight) and leave those times available.

- Determine whether you can use post-teaching downtime as a time for grading or for class preparation. Devoting certain days to teaching and others to your work can be an effective division of time.

- Schedule your blocks of time with natural breaks to end them (e.g., meals, sleep, scheduled activities like exercise). This will make it easier for you to stick to your schedule and to keep your activities distinct.

Monday	Tuesday	Wednesday	Thursday	Friday
8—11 Grad. courses	8–11 Teaching prep.	8–10 Grad. courses	9–11 OFFICE HOURS	9–12 Grading time
11–5 Grad. course work	11–1 Free time!	10–12 SECTION 1	11–1 Free time!	12–1 Free time!
	1–5 Grad. course work	12–1 Lunch	1–5 Grad. courses and course work	1–5 Misc. work time
		1–3 SECTION 2 3–5 class prep./ notes on teaching		

Coordinating Teaching and Personal Schedules

In graduate school, you must learn to be a student *and* a teacher and still feel like you have time to be human.

Sharing the Burden

You owe it to your students to be prepared for every class, to be familiar with all of the material, and to take them and their work seriously. You also owe it to yourself to take advantage of opportunities to do less, not more, work. Here are a few suggestions.

- Ask your students to prepare review questions before an exam and help them work through the answers as opposed to developing a review sheet for them.
- Ask your students to take responsibility for giving presentations to their classmates at the end of the semester.
- Ask several students to come to class prepared with a discussion question about a text so that you do not have to devise all of the questions.
- Invite a guest speaker.

Employing such strategies will significantly lighten your teaching load because you will be asking students to take partial responsibility for leading the class. And it may even improve your teaching as students become more active learners.

Scheduling Due Dates

If you have control over when your students will hand in papers, exams, or problem sets, try to schedule these at times when you will not be working on significant papers, exams, or problem sets of your own. Then schedule uninterrupted grading times

"When I first started as a teaching assistant, I was all too willing to accommodate the schedules of my students, even if it was inconvenient for me. I had one student who could never make my regularly scheduled office hours but who often wanted to meet. I would usually agree to meet at a time he suggested, even if I knew that it meant walking from one side of campus to the other and then back again after our meeting. I am now more careful about when I agree to meet with students. If you take a few extra minutes, you can often find a time that is convenient for both of you."

and uninterrupted work times for yourself throughout the week; protect those times jealously! Do not schedule meetings with students or professors during your work times; do not let yourself grade during your work times. And if you finish grading early in a scheduled block of grading time, give yourself the rest of the scheduled block as free time.

▣ Self-Preservation

You would not be a graduate student if you did not hold yourself to high standards in your academic life. Many graduate students feel that they should be as good at teaching as they are at learning. It is easy to forget that you have spent at least 16 years of full-time work honing your skills as a student. It is also easy to forget that if you stay in academia, you will spend your career perfecting your skills as a teacher; even the most talented and experienced teachers learn and develop new skills all the time.

Enjoy Your Successes

Be sure to recognize things that are going well in your classes and take credit for them. Do not assume that you are responsible only for the things that go poorly.

Expect and Accept Your Failures

Things will not always go well. You will have difficulty dealing with some students. Some of your discussions will go better than others. Students will ask you questions for which you are not prepared. You will have days when not one of your students will have something helpful to contribute to the class. You will have class plans blow up in your face.

Some of the things that go wrong in your class will be a result of something the students did, some will be the result of something you did, and some will result from a misalignment of the stars. All good teachers have bad days, and there is such a thing as an awkward group of students who will not come together to learn no matter what you do. Expect that you will make mistakes and take time to figure out what went wrong. Make notes on your class plan about what happened so that if you ever use it again, you will be able to make changes. The sooner you accept that things will not always go well, the sooner you can use your mishaps to guide you to better teaching in the future.

See pages 200–2 in Chapter 9, Meta-Teaching, for more information on how to walk back into the classroom after a bad day.

Think of Teaching as a Process

Teaching is like driving. Even though you likely got your driver's license when you were 16, you are a better driver now (we hope!) than you were when you first were let out on the road. Graduate students teach because they are more familiar with the material than the undergraduates. Other than that, there is no reason why a graduate student who has never taught before should be a perfectly skilled teacher. You will continue to develop and learn as a teacher with every semester, but to begin, you will just have to take the wheel and start driving.

Appendixes

Appendix A
Sample Course Syllabus

Psychology 101
INTRODUCTORY PSYCHOLOGY

Teaching Assistant: Frances Francini
Office: Room 2301 Big Hall
Office Hours: M & Th 10–11 (If you cannot make these hours, please feel free to make an appointment.)
Psychology Dept. Phone: 555-6333 (You can leave a message.)
Email Address: fran@theuniv.edu (checked daily)

COURSE DESCRIPTION: The goal of this class is to introduce you to psychology as a field and to familiarize you with the practice, principles, research methods, and controversies of the divisions within psychology: clinical, social, cognitive, organizational, developmental, and biological.

GRADING: Your final grade will be calculated based on a semester total of 600 points:

Paper one = 100 points
Papers two and three @ 50 points each = 100 points
Multiple-choice practice questions, worth 5 points each = 60 points
Three tests, worth 100 points each = 300 points
Participation in class discussion = 40 points

A = 600–560	C+ = 479–460	D– = 379–360
A– = 559–540	C = 459–440	F = 359 and below
B+ = 539–520	C– = 439–420	
B = 519–500	D+ = 419–400	
B– = 499–480	D = 399–380	

ATTENDANCE AND PARTICIPATION: You will be allowed two absences during the semester. Your section grade will go down by 2% for each additional absence. Exceptions may be made for significant (and documented) emergencies and illnesses—a broken alarm clock does not qualify as a significant emergency (sorry). Your participation grade will be based on your contributions to class discussions and/or your demonstration of participation in the course through visits to office hours, contributions to class email discussions, etc.

GROUP PRESENTATIONS: The group presentations will be due on November 23. Each group presentation will last for about ten minutes. An informational sheet on the group presentation will be handed out in class on November 9.

PAPER: Your papers should be 4–5 pages (double-spaced) in length. More detailed descriptions of the papers will be handed out on Sept. 21. Papers will be graded down by one half-grade for every day that they are late.

PLAGIARISM: Plagiarism is the act of presenting other people's work or ideas as your own. If you are suspected of plagiarism, your work will likely be forwarded to the college's academic judiciary. Plagiarism can result in suspension or expulsion from the university. If you have any questions about how to reference material or about what constitutes plagiarism, please come see me.

SCHEDULE

Sept. 13   The Development of Psychology as a Field
             Reading: Textbook, Chapter 1

    20   Social Psychology
             Reading: Textbook, Chapters 2 & 3
             Paper assignment #1 will be handed out.

    27   Biological Psychology
             Reading: Textbook, Chapter 5
             * Bring two copies of draft of paper to section.

(And so on)

Appendix B
Lesson Plan for a Discussion Class

GOAL: Ensure that students understand findings of recent research on the neurochemical basis of aggressive behavior and explore the social and ethical implications of this kind of psychological research

LESSON: Review research readings, ask students to design studies that highlight the limits that ethical practice places upon scientific research, and explore broader ethical questions in this area

1. Class business:

   - Assign articles for next week's information exchange
   - Have each student write down a question about yesterday's lecture on an index card; collect these and ask a few people to volunteer questions (we'll talk about the others next week)

   (10–15 minutes)

2. Review of recent research on the impact of noradrenaline and serotonin on aggressive behavior (let's do this together to make sure we're all on the same page):

   - Two students at board as the classmates share ideas: one student writing list of what we know about the relationship; one writing list of what we still do not know

   (10 minutes)

3. Group activity: In groups of three, come up with a study that would elaborate on our current understanding of the relationship between noradrenaline, serotonin, and aggressive behavior but would be unethical.

   (8 minutes)

4. Discussion based on activity: Have groups share their study and their ethical concern about it.

   • Do others agree that such a study would be unethical?

   (20 minutes?)

5. More general discussion (if time):

   • Should different ethical standards be applied to human and animal research?

   • Some would argue it is not "good science" to use results from animal studies to make assertions about human behavior. Do you agree? Why or why not?

   • If a drug did exist that drastically reduced aggressive behavior in humans, should it be made available for use? If so, on whom? Under what conditions, if any, could a person be required to take the drug?

6. Wrapping up:

   • Relate student points to the next set of readings about ethical science.

   • Remind students of expectations for information exchange.

Appendix C
Lesson Plan for a Lecture Class

GOAL: Help students understand Kohlberg's stages of moral development and how they relate to real-world situations

LESSON: Begin with a lecture to briefly review the textbook descriptions of Kohlberg's stages; have students participate in moral reasoning activity; use board to match the students' examples of moral reasoning to the appropriate Kohlbergian stage.

- Class business:
  —alert students to change in date of make-up exam
  —hand back stray papers from last week

1. Review textbook definitions for each of Kohlberg's stages:

   (10 minutes)

   - Preconventional morality
   - Conventional morality
   - Postconventional morality

2. Put students into pairs, give handout, have each pair of students

   (10 minutes)

   - Decide which of the worthy students described in their handout should receive a coveted scholarship.
   - *Write out their reasons* for why they chose the student they did.

3. Each pair will share their decision and the reasoning behind their decision. Write the reasons on the board.

   (15 minutes)

4. Return to definitions of each of Kohlberg's stages, and ask students to help to match the varieties of reasoning on board to the appropriate Kohlberg stage.

(15 minutes)

5. Conclusion: Remind students that it is the nature of the moral reasoning, not the actual decision, that matters in Kohlberg's theory. Prepare students for next week's look at Carol Gilligan's response to Kohlberg's theory.

(5 minutes)

Appendix D
Annotated Text with Questions

Text:

Sexual harassment involves an (abuse) of power. Teachers always have more
institutional power than students; students sometimes have more physical
or cultural power than teachers. Sexual harassment between teachers and
students can go both ways. Instructors may be sexually harassed by students,
but it usually happens the other way around. — a warning to the audience

neg. connotations   *statement (not opinion)*

Sexual Harassment by Teaching Assistants   *the transition to more specifics*   *necessity*

You are in the position of authority with regard to your students; you (must,)
therefore, be especially careful not to abuse your power. Many teaching
assistants are close enough in age to their students that they may flirt with
the idea of having a romantic encounter with one of them. These thoughts
may be fueled by the fact that students often have crushes on their teaching
assistants. Under no circumstances should you pursue a romantic and/or
sexual relationship with a current student. In addition, you should (never)
do (anything) that might be construed by a reasonable person as a sexual
advance.

Questions:

- What tone is established with the first sentence? Which
  words jump out at you?
- How do the authors shift tone (and audience) in the second paragraph by starting with the word *you*? Why do you
  think they do that?
- Circle the language in the second paragraph that stresses
  necessity. How does this make you feel as the reader?
- How do the authors establish their authority?

- Why have the authors chosen to present the perspectives of both teachers and students?
- The organization reflects a movement from general observations to specific advice. How would the text read differently if it started with the second paragraph?

Appendix E
Guidelines for an Essay Workshop

Workshopping in Groups[1]

The goal of a peer workshop is to help the writer of an essay see what aspects of the essay still need work and to suggest possible approaches to the essay's revision. It is a time for the writer to work directly with the audience to make the essay as effective as possible.

Readers: You are the audience of this essay, and it is your task to help the author achieve his or her desired reaction to the essay. The workshop is *not* a time for you to read your response verbatim to the author; he or she can read the response later. The workshop is a time to *talk* with the author about your reaction to the essay, about the author's concerns, about areas you think need more development, about ideas you did not understand, etc.

As the audience, you should tell the author how the text "reads." Your response to an essay cannot be "wrong" because it is your opinion. It is helpful to the author to know how readers are responding, and he or she can decide whether or not to revise the essay to avoid or heighten this reaction.

Focus on the essay's argument and main ideas. Talking about the argument of an essay is more valuable than talking about the details of the prose because after revision of the argument, the prose of the text may be drastically altered. Ask yourself, what are the two or three things I can say which will help this essay the most? Matters such as purpose, tone, perspective, large-scale organization, and logic should be first on the agenda. Do not ask the writer to accept or reject any suggestion on the spot. You are simply suggesting possible alternatives, which the writer can mull over.

---

[1]Inspired in part from Jack Rawlins, *The Writer's Way*, 2d ed. (Boston: Houghton Mifflin, 1992).

Authors: Most of us have trouble responding well to criticism of our own writing. Writing can be a personal act, and an essay can become an object of affection and of almost parental pride. It can be difficult to separate criticism of the essay from criticism of our ideas and from criticism of ourselves.

Approach the workshop with a positive mind-set; remember that the session is for your benefit and will help you improve the essay before it is graded. You can set the tone for the workshop; if you seek out constructive advice, you will usually elicit it.

Try to avoid becoming overly defensive; if you argue away all your readers' reactions and suggestions, you defeat the purpose of a workshop. If you find yourself feeling defensive, take control of the conversation and start asking questions about the aspect of the essay—questions you know will help you in revision. Create a situation in which you feel your readers are working *with* you on the paper, not against you.

Do not feel, however, that you must accept every suggestion from your readers unquestioningly. Sometimes your readers' responses will be contradictory or confusing. Ask them to explain or elaborate. You are the one with an intended purpose for the essay, and only you can accomplish it. Your readers can help you see where you have gone astray, especially if you explain your goals to them.

Group Dynamics: You will be working in groups of three. Do not work from your written responses for the in-class workshop; instead, use your copy of the draft (which should already have your comments on it) as the basis for discussion. It often works well if the writer controls the discussion, at least in the beginning, but if the writer does not feel comfortable with this role, one of the readers should get the ball rolling. Your group should spend about twenty minutes on each paper, which should be enough time for you to discuss each paper thoroughly.

If you are looking for some structure, here are a few basic questions you can use to guide your discussion.

1. What did the readers see as the essay's argument? What was the author's intended argument? If these are different, what has gone awry?

2. Is the argument focused enough? Is it developed enough? In other words, does the author need to push his or her ideas one more step?

3. Does the author fully support and develop the argument? Do all the main ideas support the argument? Do any need more detail?

4. Is the organization of the essay clear? Are there transitions between ideas/paragraphs? Are the author's ideas easy to follow?

5. Are there any paragraphs which do not have a clear function within the essay as a whole?

6. Are there any generalizations in the essay you thought were unsupported or weak?

7. Was the author's tone in the essay effective? Was his or her diction (word choice, style, etc.) appropriate to the subject?

8. Did the introduction get your attention? How is the transition from the introduction into the argument? Does the conclusion do more than regurgitate what already has been said?

9. Does the author have any remaining questions?

Appendix F
Guidelines for Writing a
Peer Response

Peer Reviews

1. Read through your classmate's essay once without stopping. It is important to get the big picture of the essay before you focus on the individual parts.

2. Reread the essay with a pencil/pen in hand and make notes in the margins or between the lines with your thoughts or questions about the author's ideas, organization, or anything else you notice. Note: this stage of the writing process is not the time to be proofreading, because the author probably will make major changes to the entire paper, not to mention the individual words and sentences. Focus instead on the paper's organization, paragraph structure, supporting details, transitions, etc. You will be using this marked-up draft in the workshop discussion, and you will be giving it to the author.

3. Respond to the following set of questions. You can either frame the response as a letter to the author, making sure that you cover all this ground, or you can write a coherent paragraph or more about each aspect of the paper. Your response should be 1–1½ pages long, single-spaced. Make your comments as constructive and specific as you can so that the author can use them to improve the paper. Provide positive feedback along with constructive suggestions. Print out two copies (one for the author and one for the instructor) and bring them to the workshop; put your name on top and then the title of the paper and the author.

A. Argument: Restate the paper's argument and then evaluate its effectiveness. For example, you can discuss whether you found the argument interesting and/or provocative or whether it does not push far enough beyond the fairly obvious. If you had trouble identifying the argument—perhaps because there are multiple arguments or the paper remains in generalities—help the author see where you had problems.

B. What's Working? Help the author see what is working really well in the paper, so that he/she is sure not to lose that in revision.

C. What's Not Working Yet? Help the author see where you struggled when reading the paper, perhaps because a point isn't clear or evidence is not clearly related to the overall argument or the organization is hard to follow, etc.

In these general categories, here are a few things you should be sure to cover:

- **Evidence:** Which claims need more evidence, more detail, or more support in order to be convincing? Where is evidence not clearly linked to specific claims? Where are there generalizations without specific evidence?

- **Detail:** Where would more detail usefully illustrate an author's point?

- **Organization:** Can you explain the organization of the paper in a way that makes sense? If not, where did you get lost, and how might this be rectified? Identify any parts of the paper that you thought were repetitive or unnecessary.

- **Introduction:** Does the introduction make you want to keep reading? If so, could you also determine the focus as well as perhaps the argument of the paper? Can you suggest ways to make the introduction clearer and/or more interesting?

- **Conclusion:** In what way does the conclusion do more than regurgitate the argument of the paper? Could it do more, or should it do less?

Appendix G
Sample Letters of Recommendation

A. For an excellent student whom you know well

January 17, 2011

It is a true pleasure for me to write this letter of recommendation for Sandra Garcia, who was my student in Sociology 115, "Introduction to Sociology," in the winter term of 2010. Sandra is, without question, one of the four or five most outstanding students I have taught at Big State University in six semesters of teaching.

Sandra is a careful and creative thinker with an eye for details and a devotion to logic, which serves her well both in the sciences and outside them. She has the terrific ability to draw on her own experience and observations to develop thoughtful opinions on a variety of issues. Sandra already knew she wanted to major in biology when she took my course, but this did not diminish her intellectual curiosity about the topics we covered in introductory sociology. Her regular contributions to full-class discussions provided insight both for her peers and for me as an instructor.

Sandra was also invaluable in small-group interaction with her peers. Without my asking, she took on the responsibility of helping her classmates consolidate vast amounts of information into coherent sets of ideas, and she quickly became a study group leader. In addition, Sandra was very generous with her time and energies. I remember her meeting individually with a student from Thailand several times before the final exam to help him master all the material in a foreign tongue.

Sandra breaks the "scientist" stereotype with her writing: she was the best writer in the two sections I taught that semester. And what was perhaps even more impressive was that she took the task of improving her writing as or more seriously than any other student in the class. One of her essays was later published in the annual magazine of the best undergraduate essays written in sociology.

Sandra is not only an excellent student, but she is also personally delightful. She is as comfortable with herself as she is engaging, pleasant, and humorous. As I got to know Sandra over the semester, I became only more impressed by the wide range of her abilities—and by her modesty about them. She is also an accomplished musician and scientist, both of which she does with a passion rare in undergraduates.

I wholeheartedly recommend Sandra as a prospective medical school student. In fact, I can think of few students whom I would recommend as highly. She will add a great deal to any incoming medical school class. I can also envision Sandra as a highly competent and caring doctor someday, which I say as a high compliment indeed. Please contact me if there is anything else I can do on her behalf.

Sincerely,

Peter Severs, M.A.

Peter Severs, M.A.
Graduate Student Instructor

B. For a good student that you do not know well

5 January 2011

I am pleased to recommend Natasha Kincaid for admission to the Teacher Education Program. Natasha was my student in Biology 210 (Cell Biology), and she proved to be a model student. She is extremely conscientious about her work and about attending class and lab. Because of her hard work, she consistently scored in the top ten percent on all the exams and problem sets. Her work demonstrates an attention to detail and an ability to integrate material to create larger frameworks for discussion.

Natasha made intelligent and insightful contributions during full-class discussion, but it was in lab that her enthusiasm and teaching abilities shone. After the first week, she became the leader of her lab group, and I would often see her patiently explaining a procedure or a concept to her lab mates (and often those in the neighboring lab group as well!). She took the initiative to organize and lead class reviews before the exams, and other students told me afterward how helpful these sessions were.

I believe that Natasha's strong academic abilities and her clear dedication to teaching make her a very strong candidate for the Teacher Education Program. If there are any questions I can answer, please feel free to contact me.

Mrinal Mukherjee
Graduate Student Instructor

C. For an average student

30 June 2011

I am pleased to write a letter of recommendation for George Gump as part of his application to dentistry school. As George's instructor for Math 235 (Set Theory), I found him to be a conscientious and hardworking student. The course was not required for George's major; he took it out of intellectual interest, and he approached the material with the same curiosity and determination that he applies in biology and medicine.

George's work on the problem sets and exams demonstrated careful attention to detail. He was also able and willing to articulate his questions about the more abstract notions of set theory, a genuine asset for many of his classmates and the class dynamic as a whole.

George is an extremely personable young man who seems equally comfortable with his peers and with faculty. He has talked with me about his goal of becoming a dentist, and I have enjoyed seeing such enthusiasm in an undergraduate about a professional career. George's commitment to the field and his hard work in pursuing his goals will serve him well in dentistry school.

Please contact me if I can answer any further questions.

Sincerely,

Kelly Atkins, Ph.D.

Kelly Atkins, Ph.D.
Lecturer

Appendix H
Midterm Feedback Form

Midterm Feedback Form

You can use a selection from the following questions for a midterm feedback form.

1. In what ways would you adjust the reading assignments for the second half of the term?

2. How could our discussions of the readings be made more helpful and relevant to your own work?

3. For the next two long papers, how much freedom in the choice of topic would you like, compared to earlier assignments?

4. How could I make my comments on your papers more helpful for you?

5. What changes would you like to see in our in-class discussions?

6. Have you found keeping a journal to be a useful activity? How often do you think you should write entries, and how often should I read them?

7. What suggestions do you have for making peer writing workshops more effective?

8. Please complete the following.

   I would like to see more time devoted to:

   I would like to see less time devoted to:

   I am still confused about:

9. Please comment on any other aspects of the course that are on your mind.

Appendix I
Coursework Release Form

BIG CITY UNIVERSITY

Department of History

Coursework Release Form

To the Student:

Papers you write for this course are your property, and you have legal control over whether you wish your instructor to be able to use your work in published articles, in a teaching portfolio, and/or as a teaching aid in future classes. Signing this form will give your instructor permission to use copies of your papers in the ways you specify.

I hereby give my consent to _____
 (Name of Instructor)
to use my essays submitted for _____
 (Name of Course)
during _____ for the purpose of
 (Semester and Year)
publication, for inclusion in a teaching portfolio, or as a teaching aid in future classes.

I would like the following credit for my work:

_____ I prefer to be named as author.

_____ I prefer to remain anonymous.

_____ I am willing either to be credited or to remain anonymous at the instructor's discretion.

I understand that granting or not granting this release will not affect my grade in this course.

_____

Signature

_____

Date

_____
_____
_____

Permanent Address and Phone Number

Index